DANCE FOR SPORTS

DANCE FOR SPORTS

A Practical Guide

Margo K. Apostolos

OXFORD
UNIVERSITY PRESS

OXFORD
UNIVERSITY PRESS

Oxford University Press is a department of the University of Oxford. It furthers
the University's objective of excellence in research, scholarship, and education
by publishing worldwide. Oxford is a registered trade mark of Oxford University
Press in the UK and certain other countries.

Published in the United States of America by Oxford University Press
198 Madison Avenue, New York, NY 10016, United States of America.

Library of Congress Cataloging-in-Publication Data
Names: Apostolos, Margo K., author.
Title: Dance for sports : a practical guide / Margo K. Apostolos.
Description: New York, NY, United States of America : Oxford University Press, [2019] |
Includes bibliographical references and index.
Identifiers: LCCN 2018009728 (print) | LCCN 2018024431 (ebook) |
ISBN 9780190621414 (Updf) | ISBN 9780190621421 (Epub) |
ISBN 9780190621377 (cloth : alk. paper) | ISBN 9780190621384 (pbk. : alk. paper)
Subjects: LCSH: Dance. | Athletes—Training of. | Sports sciences.
Classification: LCC GV1588 (ebook) | LCC GV1588 .A66 2019 (print) | DDC 792.8—dc23
LC record available at https://lccn.loc.gov/2018009728

9 8 7 6 5 4 3 2 1

Paperback printed by Sheridan Books, Inc., United States of America
Hardback printed by Bridgeport National Bindery, Inc., United States of America

This book is dedicated to my lifelong friend, Steve Miller. Steve was the first coach to recognize my vision to teach dance for athletes in 1978 at California Polytechnic State University-San Luis Obispo. He has remained unconditionally loyal throughout the years. Steve motivates and brings out the best in people, through his work as a great coach and athletic director, to his position as vice president of Global Marketing at Nike, and now as CEO of Agassi Graf Holdings. His loyalty and diligence have kept me "en pointe" with my writing.

This book is a collaborative effort with Steve, as he has read every version and revision of my many manuscripts, offering constant motivation and inspiration. He remained completely honest, genuinely caring, and continually supportive throughout the many hours of editing, advising, and forming the shape of this book by providing the intuition of the coach.

Steve Miller has been the voice of reason throughout most of my career in both dance and sport. His knowledge and experience as a coach and athlete have provided the insight that was critical in the writing of this book. Steve's academic background in English and English literature combined with his uncanny common sense provided the perfect sounding board for ideas and decisions throughout the work. This enthusiastic, charismatic, and candidly honest coach is my friend and trusted colleague for life and is truly for me the "godfather of Dance for Sports." Thank you for everything, Steve.

CONTENTS

FOREWORD

A young girl's vision is uncluttered by her environment and experience. Her eye captures pictures that are indelible, processed clearly and unfiltered. She's absolutely definitive regarding the content of the athletic images she observes. Associations begin to form . . . "it all seems so effortless: it's beautiful to watch; it's almost as if they are dancing!"

And so the journey began.

The first time I met Margo was in San Luis Obispo, California. It was her first day as an educator at California Polytechnic University. I was immediately drawn to her passion for seemingly all things, especially life; the depth of her obvious academic curiosity; and most of all, her uncanny ability to clearly articulate her vision. We were instantly "joined at the hip!" The moment she suggested that dance could be an alternative enhancement to our Olympic-level track and field training I immediately stood at attention, grinned from ear to ear, and just nodded my head up and down.

Her words and vision proved prophetic. Margo was "spot on" and I simply came along for the ride. The direct benefits that my athletes derived from her dance intervention were immediate, obvious, and powerful. Range of motion improved dramatically; running mechanics were greatly enhanced; all of my athletes reveled in the freedom of movement and the spatial awareness that dance for sport generously guided and provided.

That young female visionary has been profoundly affecting athletes at every competitive level for decades.

Steve Miller
CEO
Agassi Graf Holdings
BILT by Agassi & Reyes
Andre Agassi Foundation for Education,
1120 N. Town Center Drive,
Suite 160, Las Vegas, NV 89144

THE BACKSTORY

DANCE FOR SPORTS

Human movement is the common denominator between dance and sport, with visible similarities in training and performance. Actually, the program that came to be called Dance for Sports began when I became aware of the art in the sport and the sport in the dance. This book unfolds with early visions of bodies in motion through the journey from a child's imagination to the reality of training athletes in a variety of sports. Practice-based research in dance and sport started at California Polytechnic State University in San Luis Obispo, California (Cal Poly-SLO), became refined at Stanford University, and flourished at the University of Southern California. Using dance techniques for sport activities involves the transfer of training between dance and sport skills. This book explores the correlation of dance and sport.

Dance for Sports (DFS) came to fruition in San Luis Obispo, California, in 1978. Steve Miller, Cal Poly-SLO track and field coach, encouraged my work in dance classes for athletes. We developed the course titled "Dance for Sports" for all students, and Coach Miller's middle-distance runners enrolled in this experimental class. The working hypothesis was that dance training would enhance athletic performance. We found that the runners benefited from the dance class with an apparent increase in flexibility, although no standardized measurements were conducted. Steve's teams went on to win multiple state and national championships, encouraging our continuation of the dance class with athletes. In addition, the athletes enjoyed the experimental class.

In the early 1980s at Stanford University, I developed a framework to examine the training techniques and theoretical basis of DFS as part of my doctoral program with Stanford diving coach Rick Schavone. Together, we identified the variables of rhythmic and kinesthetic awareness that were unique in dance training. The principles of sport specificity and transfer of training provided a foundation for using these variables in working with a variety of sports. An early research study included a class, Dance for Divers, described in the appendix to this book.

The majority of the work has been accomplished at the University of Southern California between 1986 and 2016. During the years while I was developing these techniques, numerous athletes who participated in DFS have gone on to successful careers in the Olympics, the National Football League (NFL), the National Basketball Association (NBA), the Women's National Basketball Association (WNBA), and other international sport teams. My dance students include athletes from football, track and field, basketball, baseball, volleyball, tennis, swimming, diving, water polo, rowing, soccer, lacrosse, and golf. At USC, the athletes attend elective dance classes with students from various majors around the campus. My intent is for the dance skills to reinforce their athletic maneuvers by increasing their rhythmic and kinesthetic awareness. The movements in dance were often tailored to meet the demands of a specific sport and reinforce movement patterns from that sport.

The specific objectives of my program of DFS are as follows:

* To increase rhythmic awareness
* To enhance individual kinesthetic awareness
* To enjoy dance as cross training for sport
* To explore creative thinking with relation to movement
* To explore improvisational movement
* To promote relaxation, meditation, and mindfulness
* To relate to specific sports by utilizing sport similarity in movement
* To transfer the training from dance to the sport experience

A number of components overlap in the physical training of both sport and dance. These include flexibility, strength, coordination, agility, balance, and timing. Spatial awareness, temporal awareness, and reaction time influence both dance and sport performance and training. The objectives in DFS common to the physical training of both dance and sport include these:

* To increase the ease and efficiency of movement
* To increase simple coordination
* To locate, strengthen, and manipulate the body center (core) in the development and control of body placement
* To control and maintain proper breath control
* To strengthen body parts in isolation

- To develop overall flexibility and increase the range of joint movement
- To increase psychomotor development through a concentrated effort of learning simple sequences of dance and step combinations

Dance offers the athlete a very unique and complementary experience for sport training sessions. The dance training program for athletes evolved over many years of teaching to include a variety of styles, forms, and specific exercises from modern dance, jazz dance, and ballet. DFS exercises include techniques of floor work, ballet barre, flexibility stretching, agility, and coordination sequences. Athletes enjoy performing simple choreography with step progressions and combinations along with musical accompaniment.

BOXING, BASEBALL, AND BALLET

My exposure to dance and sport began in my childhood growing up in Chicago, Illinois. My early visions relating sport and dance were found in sport icons Muhammad Ali, Ernie Banks, Juan Marichal, Sandy Koufax, and dance legends Rudolf Nureyev and Margot Fonteyn. Any boundaries of dance and sport were blurred in my mind. Actually, I saw the art of sport and the sport of dance as having a common denominator: human movement. The bodies in motion appeared similar and captivating.

The late Muhammad Ali (then known as Cassius Clay) was a vision of beauty in motion. Thus begins the vision of seeing dance in sport. His sculpted body resembled a chiseled work of art moving with grace, elegance, strength, and efficiency. He moved with the rhythm of a dancer in an almost artistic performance, making boxing moves appear dancelike and choreographed. Musical accompaniment was not necessary to see and feel Ali's timing in the patterns of his steps and swings. The young Ali was light on his feet, agile in his rhythmic movements, and fluid in his actions with a flow capturing the attention and cheers of the audience. In his own words, he "floats like butterfly and stings like a bee."[1]

Another early influence from sport was the late Ernie Banks, a popular shortstop for the Chicago Cubs. A shortstop often initiates the exciting double play, beautiful to watch and scored as 6 (shortstop)-4 (second baseman)-3 (first baseman). The double play 6-4-3 is executed with quick footwork and pinpoint timing resembling the rhythm of a dancelike quick step known as a "chasse" or step, together, step. Ernie Banks moved with wonderful agility and smooth precision in the infield. His quick footwork and coordinated throwing arm made a double play look effortless. Fielding a ball and making a quick throw to second base has a fluid pattern, at times appearing to be choreography in the infield. My childhood dream was to play shortstop for the Chicago Cubs when they moved Ernie Banks to first base.

Two opposing pitchers of the era stood out: Juan Marichal of the San Francisco Giants and Sandy Koufax of the Los Angeles Dodgers. Although they faced my beloved Cubs, I was mesmerized with their pitching styles. Juan Marichal had a pace and motion that was fluid with a calming effect on the spectator. From the wind-up to the delivery, Marichal's smooth acceleration appeared to be almost liquid. On the pitching mound, he executed an extraordinary high kick with somewhat of a theatrical flair, making it resemble a dance grand battement. Another pitcher, Sandy Koufax, was efficient, effortless, and seamless with his action. Koufax's precision, fluidity, and timing captured the spectator with each perfect pitch. There was both grace and precision in his actions, reminiscent of the carriage of the dancers' arms or port de bras.

These athletes created a visualization of rhythm that I saw and felt in my body. This captivated my curiosity driven by a naïve intuition. Sport was beautiful to watch. The fluid movements of these iconic athletes—Ali, Banks, Marichal, and Koufax—were the idealization of beauty and grace to me, distinct and unforgettable in the eyes of a child. However, my introduction to dance came while watching two dancers on a popular television variety show hosted by Ed Sullivan.

Ballet superstars of the same era, Rudolf Nureyev and Margot Fonteyn, partnered together dancing with beauty, rhythm, and grace. As a child, watching the dancers was mesmerizing, aesthetically pleasing, and physically powerful. The strength, agility, coordination, timing, and rhythm of the dance performers captured the attention and imagination of the audience. It was neither boxing nor baseball, but the movements in ballet had a similarity to sport. The human body is the vehicle for performance in both dance and sport with the athletes and the dancers utilizing the physical elements of strength, agility, coordination, timing, balance, and rhythm. Margot Fonteyn was strong but graceful, and her movements had an abstract similarity to movements in sport. In my naïve eyes, Rudolf Nureyev and Margot Fonteyn appeared to be athletes dressed in fancy costumes with musical accompaniment.

The beautiful ballet movements resembled the athleticism observed in boxing and baseball. The dancers moved to the sounds of the music with the musculature of athletes. Their dance movements became the visualization of the music that accompanied the performance. Muhammad Ali's footwork in the ring, Ernie Banks's agility in the infield, Juan Marichal's kick, and Sandy Koufax's effortless arm on the mound each demonstrate specific rhythms in time and space similar to actions of Nureyev and Fonteyn on stage. The movements in dance have a similarity to movement in sport. The setting and costumes were different but the actions of the human bodies were similar.

The grace and fluidity of human motion flows rhythmically—with music on stage or without music on the field and in the ring—in the performances of both athletes and dancers. The bodies of the dancers resemble sculptures, and the physical elements of strength, flexibility, coordination, balance, agility, and timing were similar to those displayed by athletes, but displayed in an aesthetic form. Could Nureyev ever have been fighting in a ring with Ali or Koufax dancing with Fonteyn? As a child, I did not know the boundaries of disciplines and could only imagine those possible matchups. Dance for me was like watching sport on a stage.

A catalyst in my pursuit of linking dance and sport came in 1977 with a book titled *The Ultimate Athlete* by George Leonard, popular in the 1970s when a wave of mind and body study developed at the Esalen Center in Big Sur, California. The message of his book was the power of awareness in the mind, body, and spirit. Leonard saw the inner processes and sensations of the individual manifested into movement becoming the dance. The dancer was identified as the "ultimate athlete," with dance as the universal training that applied to all movement. That statement propelled my mission to bring dance and sport training together.

Seemingly, Leonard's book endorsed my childhood vision of linking sport and dance and bringing boxing, baseball, and ballet into the same category, thus, confirming that dancers were athletes. The message of *The Ultimate Athlete* identifies physical activity as vital to life, with dance as a vehicle of training and the ultimate athlete being the dancer. My career became devoted to finding the dance in the sport, the sport in the dance, and sharing those benefits with both athletes and dancers.

A focus on rhythmic and kinesthetic awareness are unique elements experienced in dance classes. Dance training works specifically with rhythms and body awareness for the individual dancer in mastery of dance techniques. While athletic training is sport specific, dance offers the athlete a cross-training experience with sport similarity. Dance for athletes is no longer the image of the football player in ballet but rather a variety of dance styles merging with a variety of sports. Dance, as cross training, offers a complementary training technique for the in season or off-season in sport.

ACCIDENTAL ATHLETE

The study of the science of human movement with applications to the art of dance translates into a teaching style that fostered the growth of DFS incorporating art and science in the exercises. Sport skills complemented my dance training and dance training complemented my sport activities through the similarity in human movements. I could not separate the dance from the sport in my own activities.

The scientific background of my undergraduate studies included exercise physiology, kinesiology, biomechanics, anatomy, and motor learning with the fundamental movements of both dance and sport as the common denominator. The curriculum introduced many sports and various dance styles at Southern Illinois University-Carbondale. A variety of both team and individual sports were part of the curriculum and included technique, training, teaching, coaching, and officiating at a variety of sports with the simultaneous study in performance, choreography and production of dance. The scientific analysis of movement, in dance and sport, reduced the elements of movement to mechanics and anatomy. The study of the science of human movement with applications to the art of dance reinforced my teaching style fostering the growth of Dance for Sports.

My first teaching position at the Chicago suburban Glenbard North High School included teaching dance and physical education, and coaching tennis and gymnastics. My dancing continued with jazz, modern, and ballet coupled with sport activities in gymnastics, tennis, swimming, running, cycling, rowing, and fencing. The participation in sports enhanced my dance training, performance, and teaching through an increased movement vocabulary and experience. Dance and sport became integral training throughout my graduate studies at Northwestern University.

My experience as an athlete, coach, and teacher of many sports has given me insight into the needs of the athlete. Through this experience and exposure in sports I have developed an understanding and trust with both the coach and the athlete. Athletes and dancers share many commonalities but they also work differently. You could say that I have experienced "both sides of the mirror" and continue to find dance in all movement. My world continues to see the dance in the sport and the sport in the dance. Sport skills complement my dance training and dance training complements my sport activities through the similarity in human movements.

Athletes influenced my childhood imagination with visions leading to a career in dance. The rhythm and footwork of a boxer, the agility and timing of a shortstop, the flexible high kick of one baseball pitcher, and the fluid efficiency and precision of another were the movements caught by my still naïve eyes. Yet watching the beauty and grace of ballet led me to choose dance as my passion and profession. My academic career spans more than forty years to include teaching dance, coaching, and teaching sports with continued research in Dance Medicine and robotics.

> If only one subject were to be required in school, it should be, in my opinion, some form of dance—from nursery school through PhD. I can't say that a dancer is the ultimate athlete. I am quite certain however, that the ultimate athlete is the dancer.
> George Leonard, *The Ultimate Athlete*, p. 238

ACKNOWLEDGMENTS

This book is the product of the continued collaboration with Steve Miller, fittingly named the "godfather of Dance for Sports." From the early days at Cal Poly-San Luis Obispo and throughout the entire process of this book, Steve has been instrumental. I am forever grateful for my treasured friend and colleague. Steve's longtime administrative assistant Evy Nickell was pivotal in keeping our ongoing communications on schedule throughout the writing of this book.

My sincere gratitude goes to my editor Norm Hirschy and Oxford University Press for their time and patience throughout the development of the manuscript for this book. I am deeply appreciative of the anonymous peer reviewers of Oxford University Press and Assistant Editor, Lauralee Yeary for their helpful comments and suggestions in the early stages of the process, Alyssa Russell in OUP Marketing, and my diligent project manager, Felshiya Bach. The beautiful work of photographer Rose Eichenbaum highlights former USC athletes Tatyana Obukhova McMahon and Chris Willson in selected Dance for Sport exercises. USC Kaufman Dean Robert Cutietta contributed the musical notation for the high jump sequence in Chapter 3. The Video Companion is provided by Dawn Stoppiello of Troika Ranch and features former USC athlete and professional boxer Gerald (El Gallo Negro) Washington.

Many athletes and coaches have contributed to the growth and refinement of Dance for Sports throughout the years. The support and encouragement in the development of this work from the athletic departments of the University of Southern California and Stanford University is greatly appreciated. My colleagues at the University of Southern California have recognized and encouraged this work for many years. A deep gratitude to coaches Dick Gould and Ron Allice for believing in my work, and my former student Troy Polamalu.

A majority of this book was written on the second floor of the Fairchild Library on the California Institute of Technology (Caltech) campus. The support of my Caltech and Jet Propulsion Laboratory (JPL) friends has kept me going throughout the writing of this book. The Silicon Valley Four Seasons Hotel provided a tranquil setting for the occasional writer's block.

My Dance Medicine colleagues at the Cedars-Sinai Department of Orthopaedics and Physical Therapy encouraged the documentation of this work with their ongoing support. A special thank you to my brilliant and caring doctor, Cedars-Sinai Surgical Oncologist Allan W. Silberman, MD for keeping me healthy for over thirty years and his reminder to use "common sense." My close circle of friends and family continue to surround me with love and support throughout my adventures. My late uncle, Dr. Stothe P. Kezios, taught me the importance of the continual pursuit of knowledge and remains my everlasting inspiration. The kindness, laugher, and generosity of my late brother, Don, continues to guide me each day.

Finally, the Chicago Public School System, Southern Illinois University- Carbondale, the Chicago Public Library, and the Chicago Park District provided the resources for my dreams to come to fruition. The foundation provided by these public institutions laid the foundation for my academic growth and career in education.

DANCE FOR SPORTS

INTRODUCTION

Dance for Sports: A Practical Guide serves as a primer for coaches and athletes to help them understand the values of dance training. Athletes from a variety of sports benefit from the complementary movement training of dance. Many of my former students have become Olympians, professional athletes, coaches, teachers, and mentors. My work began over forty years ago, when dance and sport were often considered separate activities. This duality may not seem extraordinary in the world of today's dance competitions and conventions, but many years ago a stark contrast existed between the notion of "winning" in sport and "expression" in dance. Times have changed this perception of dance and competition.

Dancers deal with competition regularly through auditions. With a successful audition, someone will "win" the place in the show or with the dance company. The popular television show, *Dancing with the Stars* (*DWTS*) demonstrates the correlation between dance and sports, with many celebrity contestants representing a variety of sports. In *DWTS*, the athletes perform on the dance floor with precision and grace, often winning the popular dance competition. Yes, athletes can dance. Even the National Football League relaxed the ruling for celebrations to allow expressive dancing in the end zone. Freedom of expression and movement is a spontaneous response for the athletes after they score. This National Football League (NFL) ruling includes dancing solo, with a partner, and even with the ball to celebrate on the field following scoring.

The book begins with The Backstory, a personal recollection of my early influences in sport and dance. My naïve observations of boxing, baseball, and ballet were the beginning of my career in the application of dance training to sport. Since my early visions of athletes and dance, the comparison has shifted from curiosity to reality. The movement similarities between dance and sport are obvious, with the human body a vehicle for performance. Seeing the "dance in the sport" and the "sport in the dance" led to my practice-based work in training athletes. *Dance for Sports* emerged from this discovery.

The book is divided into three sections: Part I: The Framework of Dance for Sports, Part II: Mind and Body Fitness, and Part III: Beyond the Dance. The Framework of Dance for Sports begins with the principles of sport specificity and the transfer of training between sport and dance. Rhythmic awareness and kinesthetic awareness are variables in dance training. Those unique variables impact both sport specificity and transfer of training in sport. Mind and Body Fitness discusses the additional benefits of dance including creativity, improvisation, and dance as cross training for all sports. Finally, Beyond the Dance examines philosophical thoughts in sport and dance with a look at athletes in Ancient Greece. The emphasis on music and dance in the training of those Hellenic athletes is influential in my thought and work. The union of body, mind, and spirit contributes to the total development of the individual in Dance for Sports (DFS) training. The practice-based exercises outlined in this book introduce the benefits of dance to coaches and athletes.

DFS training highlights the ability of the teacher to relate dance skills to specific sports, thus creating individualized training for athletes whether in- or off-season. The ability to understand the various sports and speak the language of athletes and coaches aids in the success of teaching dance to athletes. Each sport has its own rules, regulations, skills, venues, and training methods. The dance studio provides a neutral setting for all sports, with music an integral part of the training. The key element in DFS is the integration of dance elements into a particular sport. Success in sport rises with the mastery of specific skills, with the human body the instrument for all movement. Movement is the common denominator in DFS training.

Coaches have expressed concerns to me about affording the time in their limited practice schedules for dance training. The majority of the DFS work has been conducted as part of the academic curriculum. Athletes enroll in elective dance classes during the academic year preseason, during the season, or off-season. A typical class includes athletes from various sports, both male and female, alongside students who are not varsity athletes.

This practical guide features basic exercises that introduce athletes to dance through fundamental movements. Photographs of athletes highlight movements from the exercise sequences suitable for all sports. Chapters 1–6 present an overview of selected exercises from DFS training with explanations in sections titled Perceptions and Synthesis to Sport. My commentary on these exercises is covered in Reflections from the Mirror. The Athlete's Story features a personal side, with athletes relating to the chapter highlights. The perceptions suggest points for the athletes' personal experiences found in dance training, while the synthesis explains the value of the sequence for the coach. My reflections pinpoint valuable elements in the dance training for both the coach and the athlete from the dance teacher's perspective. Throughout the text, in the sections headed

A Point to Remember, emphatic points to ponder are highlighted, reflecting the voice of the teacher. Each chapter begins with a statement in the voice of a coach: Coach Steve Miller. His words resonate directly from the sport experience in relation to the dance.

The Athlete's Story highlights competitors from various sports including Olympic diving legend Greg Louganis; Olympic swimmer Betsy Mitchell; Olympic high jumper Jamie Nieto; Olympic sprinter Quincy Watts; champion triple jumper Tatyana Obukhova McMahon; and NFL star Devon Kennard. The stories of their success illustrate many similarities underlying dance and sport.

Chapter 1 shifts from specificity to similarity between dance and sport. A focus on the basics leads to movements adaptable to a variety of sports, both team and individual sports. This chapter features diving, baseball, basketball, and football references.

The significance of DFS training lies in the ability of the athlete to transfer dance to sport, as explained in Chapter 2. The transfer of training in motor skill performance links athletics and dance through a similarity of movement. The story of an Olympic swimmer illustrates the transfer of training with her transition from the pool to the sport of sculling.

Chapter 3 presents rhythm essential to the transfer of training between dance and sport skills. The elements of timing, tempo, pace, accent, speed, and acceleration are factors each athlete experiences through movement. All movements have a rhythm. This element, rhythm, ties movements together in the execution of sport and dance skills. In dance class, the extrinsic stimulus of music encourages the intrinsic recognition of the beat and tempo for the athletes. Examples from track and field and swimming illustrate the significance of rhythm in various sport environments: on land, in the air, and in the water.

Chapter 4 introduces kinesthetic awareness, which helps a performer to recognize body position in space and time. Rhythm is embedded in this in a personal and intimate experience. DFS training helps to increase efficiency in movement through training in body mechanics, posture, rhythm, body linkage, and individual proprioception. The release of unnecessary muscular tension and maintenance of balance through mechanics and posture aid in the efficiency of movement skills. Being aware of individual muscular motion, position in space, and weight aid in individual body awareness. In dance training, the focus is on the relationship of mind and body, emphasizing the intimacy of individual thought and action in muscle movement from posture to performance and feeling the movement. The story of an Olympic gold medalist recollects the importance of dance in his training.

The dance environment allows athletes an opportunity to shift gears from the rigors of competition and experience expressive training and individual discovery. Chapter 5 identifies the value of creativity and improvisational training for athletes. In this chapter, creativity, an element of exploration in DFS, couples with improvisational discoveries for spontaneous movement experiences The team sports of soccer and football provide examples. My former student and NFL "rookie of the year" demonstrates a combination of improvisation and kinesthetic awareness in action.

Chapter 6 on cross training highlights the importance of core training, critical in all movement. The popular DFS abdominal workout is detailed in this chapter with a video link. Dance provides a fun addition to sport training for both team and individual sports. The story of a triple jumper brings together the elements of rhythm, strength, and kinesthetic awareness in this chapter.

Chapter 7 draws from the philosophy of Ancient Greece to explore a deeper meaning of DFS. Arête, a Greek concept, involves a greater role for the athlete in society through discipline and ethics.

The works of Plato reinforce the value of dance and music in athletic training. This inclusion of music with dance training highlights the importance of rhythm and movement from the early Olympic origins.

A Glossary of Dance, Sport, and Anatomy terminology provides clarification along with a list of Further Readings for each chapter. Conversations with Champions lists the names of many coaches and athletes interviewed in preparation for this book. An Appendix presents a sport-specific class, Dance for Divers.

The Framework of Dance for Sports

/// 1 /// SEEING THE DANCE

Sport Similarity

Dance is the universal "language" for movement in all sports. It enhances and translates directly to sports specificity.

Steve Miller, "godfather of Dance for Sports"

Coach Miller saw the similarity of movements in athletes and dancers. Dance made sense to him. The similarity of movement in dance and sport was complementary in the training of his athletes. While a universal training program for all sport skills does not exist, Dance for Sports (DFS) offers an approach in dance training for a variety of sports. Dance provides training in fundamental movements that resemble and reinforce the specificity of sport through similarity in movements. This chapter features dance in the sport of diving and looks at adaptations of dance movements visible in baseball, basketball, and football.

The framework in DFS begins with sport specificity. Research supports the long-standing principle that "training for a skilled movement for one event is specific to that event."[1] This training principle is the accepted rule in sport training. Coaches and athletes know that training conditions need to resemble or be specific to the conditions in the activity. The training for a specific outcome leads to mastery of that skill. While the principle of sport specificity is critical in DFS, a similarity of movement better describes the activities in presenting dance to athletes. Actually, the similarity of fundamental movements makes dance training the perfect activity for all sports.

This chapter introduces sequences of fundamental movements for a variety of sports. The athletes' dance experience begins with the basic movement patterns of bending, stretching, and twisting. These simple exercises work with movements highlighting breath control, postural alignment, and interdependent body articulations. The sequences focus on the body linkage and individual movement perceptions. The simple dance movements in this chapter serve as a basic introduction to dance for athletes.

SPORT SIMILARITY

The similarity in dance and sport is visible in movement through shared physical components including but not limited to flexibility, agility, balance, coordination, timing, and strength. Athletes train with extensive sport-specific conditioning programs working with these physical components tailored to their sport, particular position, or task in the competition. DFS works with these similar physical components for training in the dance setting, yet with an understanding of sport specificity. Sport similarity identifies movement patterns similar in sport and dance training with a slight shift in thinking from sport specificity. Specificity applies to the specific sport while similarity includes basic elements found in all movement.

There is even similarity between dance and sport in the format of dance class that offers a comfort level to many athletes entering the dance studio. Dance classes maintain a structure often similar to that of sport; for example, both dance and sport include warm-ups and drills corresponding with dance choreography and gameplay. The nature of the warm-up varies but the preparation of the mind and the body for activity is important. Dance classes include progressions of patterns across the dance floor resembling the sport concept of drills moving up and down the field in a line formation. The culmination of class is dancing the learned choreography that focuses on a common goal, similar to the concept of a scrimmage in gameplay.

A POINT TO REMEMBER

In DFS, the dance teacher adapts the dance skills enhancing the athlete's performance without interfering with sport-specific skills. The dance teacher needs to understand the specific sport for optimal success in dance for athletes.

The adaptation of dance to sport is important, especially during the competitive season, as enhancing sport without conflict to competition and gameplay is critical for the athlete. Consider the following examples of similarity and adaptation of dance and sport. The dancer's arms and hands are often held in specific positions—for example, in ballet fifth position the arms are held overhead. A similar position of the arms and hands is used by an outfielder in baseball with a slight variation. In gameplay, an outfielder holds his arms overhead with hands facing outward while in ballet the arms are held overhead with the hands facing inward (Photo 1.1). The position of arms overhead with hands facing outward is the preparation for catching a fly ball. Clearly, the dancer's hands in fifth position would conflict with an outfielder's preparation for catching a fly ball (Photo 1.2).

Basketball players block an opponent with arms extended to their sides with elbows bent and hands up for the natural basket defensive maneuver known as "post position" (Photo 1.3). This defensive position with elbows bent and hands open is natural for the

PHOTO 1.1. Baseball outfielder preparing to catch a fly ball with hands facing outward *(Source/ author: With permission from Rose Eichenbaum Photography)*

PHOTO 1.2. Arms in ballet fifth position with hands facing inward *(Source/author: With permission from Rose Eichenbaum Photography)*

basketball player. The arms in a ballet second position would not be effective for defense on the basketball court (Photo 1.4). The ballet arms are slightly curved at the elbows with elbows below the shoulder and wrist below the elbow. With a baseball outfielder or the basketball defensive player, the athlete adapts the dance movement to the position natural for the specific sport situation. Yet the fundamentals of postural alignment and body linkage are similar in both dance and sport.

The offensive and defensive linemen in football use a variation of a basic dance position of knees slightly bent known in dance as a demi plié in second position. However,

PHOTO 1.3. Basketball player in defensive basketball "post position" with elbows bent *(Source/author: With permission from Rose Eichenbaum Photography)*

their hips remain in parallel position with their weight thrust forward and the pelvis flexed when in their stance (Photo 1.5). The dance teacher adapts the demi plié to reinforce the sport situation (Photo 1.6). The stance of a football lineman illustrates sport similarity with the variation of a dance demi plié. The similarity of positions is illustrated with these photos.

The similarity in movements is obvious, and even the coaches are able to see the dance in the sport.

The demi-plié is essential for the offensive line.

LSU Football Coach Ed Orgeron

PHOTO 1.4. Arms in ballet second position *(Source/author: With permission from Rose Eichenbaum Photography)*

SIMPLICITY OF FUNDAMENTAL MOVEMENTS

DFS begins with basic movements of bending (flexion), stretching (extension), and twisting (rotation). The simplicity of these movements allows the athletes to be aware of postural alignment. The body linkage or connection of the body forces and joint reactions contributes to fluidity in movements. A focus on these fundamental actions is a basis for movements in sport skills, dance, and activities of everyday life. These fundamental movements show the similarity in dance and sport and are quite often visible to a spectator.

THE ATHLETE'S STORY: SEEING THE DANCE

One afternoon in the summer of 1986, I was swimming and relaxing with a book on the deck of the University of Southern California (USC) swim stadium. The image of a body soaring

PHOTO 1.5. Offensive lineman on the line of scrimmage, knees bent with weight forward *(Source/author: With permission from Rose Eichenbaum Photography)*

through the air from the diving platform with repeated seamless entries into the pool caught my eye. I could not help noticing the exquisite elegance in the human form of the body in motion. The muscular body unfolded in space with rhythmic twists and turns and elongated entry into the water appearing both technically perfect and aesthetically pleasing. This diver defined the elements of beauty, strength, grace, agility, timing, fluidity, efficiency, and rhythm.

The diver executed masterful dives repeatedly throughout the afternoon. The young man climbed the ladder to the platform over and over again as he rehearsed his dives to perfection. The afternoon of diving practice by the young man demonstrated the ideal representation of sport specificity training—that is, training for a skilled movement with conditions specific to that event. I thought to myself, "This diver is magnificent to watch and looks like a future Olympian." A few minutes later that diver approached and introduced himself. He was Greg Louganis. The principle of sport specificity applies as demonstrated by the success of this multiple Olympic gold medalist. To become the world's best diver, you must dive repeatedly and consistently with training conditions specific to the activity of diving. Dance and diving share

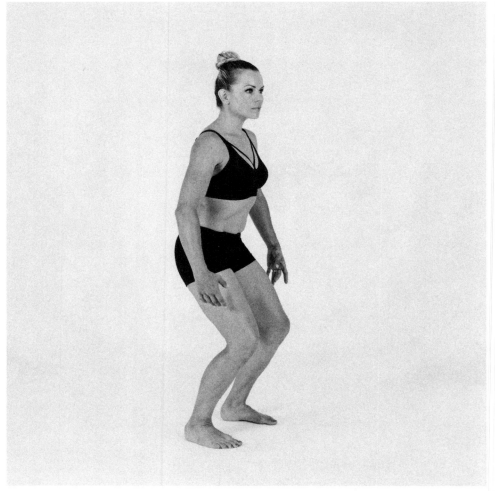

PHOTO 1.6. Parallel, second position demi plié *(Source/author: With permission from Rose Eichenbaum Photography)*

similarities in form and timing made visible in the flawless diving of Greg Louganis. Seeing the dance in his diving is obvious, as Greg is trained in dance.

> Diving is a dancer doing "ballet in the air" with pointed toes, and graceful limbs.
>
> Olympian and USC Diving Coach Hongping Li

The artistry of diving is a great example of the art of sport, showing much similarity in form and movements between dance and sport. The fundamental movements of bending, stretching, and twisting were apparent in each dive. To watch Greg's performance at the pool was to see dancing in the air with its elegance, timing, and rhythm. The beauty of a Greg Louganis dive demonstrates the combination of aesthetic and athletic perfection. The aesthetic form of a diver is an important part of the diving competition. The form of his body from takeoff to entry exhibits the blend of mechanics, motion, and beauty in sport. The execution of a dive integrates separate body parts into a single fluid movement: the whole is greater that a mere sum of the parts, beautifully illustrated by a diver in free flight—from leaving the board to entry into the water.

The effortless efficiency in the compact movement of a dive demonstrates specificity of training in sport and similarity to movements in dance. A diver commands control and timing through body awareness and rhythm, as the dive unfolds before our eyes. The simultaneous movements of interdependent body segments produce a fluidity of coordinated patterns whether on the stage or a diving platform or springboard. The simplicity of bending, stretching, and twisting becomes elegance, grace, and rhythm before our eyes. Of course, additional attention highlights an aesthetic element to the motion. The aspect of beauty is apparent in dance and recognized in sport. The dance teacher and the coach work together in DFS to produce a synthesis of aesthetics and athletics. Seeing the dance in the sport is important to the translation of dance into athletic performance.

> In sport and coaching, movement is often mechanized for competition.
>
> Retired Stanford Diving Coach Dr. Rick Schavone

An aesthetic element in the training of athletes is greater than mere mechanized movement patterns and repetitions. The beauty of a diver unfolding midair and elongating with a seamless disappearance into the water is an example of the combination of aesthetic and seemingly mechanized movement. The diver combines the elements of fundamental movements with timing and control, resulting in a vision resembling a moving sculpture. The dance elements of breath control, alignment, and fluidity are essential in the training of athletes, contributing to an aesthetic quality in movement, as seen in the sport of diving. DFS training introduces and reinforces an aesthetic element to human movement with a focus on increased body awareness.

DANCE FOR SPORTS IN PRACTICE: EXERCISES 1–4

DFS training introduces the beauty and freedom of dance movement in the relaxing atmosphere of the dance studio. A dance studio offers an open space with mirrors and musical accompaniment in an atmosphere quite different from the surfaces and competitions of gameplay. The athletes work with fundamental movements in a unique setting that sharpens their kinesthetic and rhythmic awareness, allowing them to experience movement for its own sake without the focus on winning.

DFS begins with a deep breathing sequence that aids in mental and physical centering for the athlete/dancer and serves to quiet the mind and body before performance. This simple breathing exercise is a great way for the athlete to become calm, tune into the body, and shift gears from the field to the dance studio.

EXERCISE 1: DEEP BREATHING EXERCISE FOR THE ATHLETE

(1) Lying in a supine position with arms next to the torso and palms of the hands facing upward with eyes closed, inhale deeply through the nose and mouth.
(2) Exhale, beginning with the vocalization of a "hissing" sound in a continual flow of the breath.
(3) Release the breath from the point of inhalation to the lower abdominals.
(4) Repeat the exercise four times.
(5) With each repetition, try to reach the lower abdominals.

PERCEPTIONS: EXERCISE 1

- The focus is on calming mind and body with the deepening of the exhalation.
- The deepened exhalation increases oxygenation in the body.
- Try to reach a state of self-induced relaxation.
- The spine and pelvis remain flat and level.
- An overall feeling of calm is experienced.
- The mind becomes focused on the singular aspect of the breath.
- Abdominal muscles are engaged as breath is captured on the exhalation.
- With each repetition, try to reach the lower abdominals.
- The exercise allows for shifting gears from sport to dance.

SYNTHESIS TO SPORT: EXERCISE 1

- Increase capacity of breath control.
- Sharpen focus mentally and physically.
- Reinforce postural alignment.
- Quiet the mind and connect with the body.

REFLECTIONS FROM THE MIRROR: EXERCISE 1

The deep breathing exercise quiets the mind and body and prepares the athlete for the dance experience. Quiet supine breathing is particularly helpful during the competitive season whether before or after competition. The athlete studying dance is presented with a challenging learning experience for developing independent thinking. Trained dancers learn to think in a particular way: that is, the instantaneous interpretation of visual, auditory, tactile, and spatial/directional cues encourage a different way of processing information and translating it into movement. These simple examples of movement experiences in DFS training highlight the exploration of freedom in movement for the athlete. Dance allows the athlete to express himself and provides a creative platform for his inner feelings.

Exercises 2–4 present an example of introductory sequences in DFS training. At the beginning of the progression, the athletes are sitting on the floor and facing the mirrors; they move to a supine position lying on the floor, and progress to a standing position facing the mirrors. These movements allow the athletes to notice, grasp, and experience individual body awareness, postural alignment, breath control, and body linkage. The focus of this sequence is to experience an individual sense of movement or proprioception of the muscle, ligament, and nerve connections in the body throughout these fundamental movements. The simplicity of the movements allows for a concentration of an individual movement experience for the athletes.

EXERCISE 2: STRETCHING AND BENDING SEATED ON THE FLOOR

An opening exercise introduces athletes from all sports to DFS and incorporates bending, stretching, and twisting. This introductory exercise begins with athletes facing the mirror, sitting on the floor with legs crossed. The mirror becomes a tool of immediate visual feedback for the athletes.

(1) Begin seating crossed-legged facing the mirror and inhale with arms extending overhead (Photo 1.7).
(2) Exhale, moving arms downward as the spine curves forward (Photo 1.8).
(3) Inhale and extend arms overhead, reaching then stretching to the left side (Photo 1.9).
(4) Rotate through the center with spine curved, combining steps 1, 2, and 3.

PHOTO 1.7. Arms overhead from front view with inhalation and extension *(Source/author: With permission from Rose Eichenbaum Photography)*

PERCEPTIONS: EXERCISE 2

- Experience stretching and bending in the torso.
- Experience the connection of the arms and torso throughout the movements.
- Feel the use of the breath in connection with the arm movements.
- Focus on the interdependent articulations of the torso, arms, head, and neck.

SYNTHESIS TO SPORT: EXERCISE 2

- Hips are stable in the seated position as torso bends and stretches.
- Become aware of the simplicity of bending and stretching as a foundation for sport movements.
- The emphasis is on posture, alignment, and body linkage through the fundamental movements of bending and stretching.
- Focus on arm movement connecting through the torso.
- Become aware of body linkage that connects through the torso both anterior and posterior.

PHOTO 1.8. Exhale as arms press downward and spine curves forward *(Source/author: With permission from Rose Eichenbaum Photography*

- Simultaneous movements move through a continuous path.
- Fluidity is the result of the continuous motion and transitions.

The sequence moves from the sitting position to full extension and lying on the floor in the supine position. This sequence is important to reinforce postural alignment without the force of gravity. The exercises are non-weight-bearing, often used for injury recovery.

EXERCISE 3: BENDING AND TWISTING LYING IN SUPINE POSITION ON THE FLOOR

(1) Right leg glides with bent knee and hips parallel, with pelvis stable and spine straight; repeat with left leg.
(2) Right leg bends with hip turned out and twists across center line of body (Photo 1.10).

PHOTO 1.9. Right arm extends to left with a lateral stretch of the torso *(Source/author: With permission from Rose Eichenbaum Photography)*

PHOTO 1.10. Lying supine position with bend and twist *(Source/author: With permission from Rose Eichenbaum Photography)*

(3)   Legs are straight with feet straight upward; spine remains straight with hips parallel, both knees bending; bring the heels downward toward the gluteal muscles.

PERCEPTIONS: EXERCISE 3

- Spine remains straight on the floor in supine position.
- Pelvis is level and symmetrical; body is flat in supine position.
- Focus on hip flexors, hamstrings, and quadriceps as legs glide.
- Movements of hip flexors are smooth and fluid.
- Abdominal sheath remains flat.
- Reinforce the proper alignment of joints through movement.
- Movements are nonimpact, working through joint range of movement.
- Rotate the hip inward (Photo 1.10) with spine remaining straight

SYNTHESIS TO SPORT: EXERCISE 3

- Establish straight postural alignment of the spine for body control.
- Ankle, foot, knee, and hip joints remain in alignment through movements.
- Rotate hip joints to increase range of movement.
- Joint is used through range of movement and non-weight-bearing activity.
- Movements are fluid through continuous motion.
- Focus on the body linkage through fluid movement sequences.

A progression from the floor work to standing center simplifies movement fundamentals, reinforcing correct postural alignment, balance, and fluidity in movement sequences. Proprioception is put to the test in the standing sequence of exercises, as the athlete must maintain balance throughout the entire sequence.

EXERCISE 4: BENDING, STRETCHING, AND TWISTING STANDING CENTER FLOOR

(1)   Stand facing the mirror with hips parallel, feet directly under the pelvis, with both arms overhead on the inhalation (Photo 1.11).

(2)   Both arms press downward as torso twists to the right on the exhalation. Repeat sequence to the left (Photo 1.12).

(3)   Extend legs and balance on balls of the feet with arms overhead.

PHOTO 1.11. Standing with hips parallel and arms overhead; inhalation *(Source/author: With permission from Rose Eichenbaum Photography)*

(4) Lower the heels as torso twists to the right as both arms press downward. Repeat sequence to the left.

PERCEPTIONS: EXERCISE 4

- Transfer actions from Exercise 1 (seated) and Exercise 2 (lying supine) to upright standing position.

PHOTO 1.12. Torso twist with arms pressing downward and hips forward *(Source/author: With permission from Rose Eichenbaum Photography)*

- Maintain postural alignment in standing position.
- Combine bending, stretching, and twisting of the torso in standing position.
- Establish and maintain balance on balls of the feet.
- Establish a fluid movement by connecting the actions.
- Focus movements with the direction of the movement actions.

SYNTHESIS TO SPORT: EXERCISE 4

- Be aware of sensations of postural alignment in action.
- Maintain body linkage and balance through movement sequences.
- Feel sensations of connection of movement sequences through the body linkage.
- Control the body through actions of bending, stretching, and twisting.
- Transitions between actions emphasize the fluidity in movement.
- Balance is maintained over the base of support as the torso rotates.

- Recognize internal sensations and muscular control through abdominal sheath and pelvis.
- Feel the sensations of the connection of the arms through a connection with the torso.

REFLECTIONS FROM THE MIRROR

Generally, slow music is played to encourage deep breathing at the opening of a DFS class. The basic floor work in this chapter helps the athletes to shift gears from the competition of sports to the exploration of dance. In sport-specific training, an athlete may not be asked to just slow down, breathe deeply, or relax as part of the training, thus, providing a chance for personal exploration; this is a central part of DFS. Dance experiences are also tailored to meet the needs of the athlete for injury recovery or rehabilitation.

The seated position keeps the hips grounded and fixed, as the torso bends, stretches, and twists. Sitting on the floor and facing the mirror connects arm movements into stretching and coordination activities. The body linkage focuses on the abdominal sheath throughout the entire exercise sequence. A detailed abdominal workout is included in DFS classes as the development of the abdominal sheath is crucial for all motor skills. The abdominal workout is detailed in Chapter 6 on cross training, with a video link.

The floor work highlights alignment and posture from head to toe, as the dancer lies flat on the floor without the resistance of the force of gravity. This exercise is non-weight-bearing, and the dancers listen to their bodies, breath, and feelings. Lying on the floor helps with body awareness and alignment with an introduction to the basic concepts of body articulations and fundamental movements in a very relaxed format. The importance of proper placement and form is crucial in understanding correct posture and alignment. The technical exercises help the athletes to understand the intricate work of the dancer. Simply standing and bending the knees is not taken for granted in dance, and dancers work to perfect this fundamental movement. The center floor work is critical for strength, balance, and coordination, as illustrated with Exercise 3.

The athlete transfers proper posture and alignment from the zero gravity of lying on the floor to the upright, weight-bearing standing position. The standing exercises in the center floor are performed facing the mirrors, progressing from alignment and placement in the floor sequences to a standing position, with the mirrors providing immediate visual feedback. In the standing center floor exercises, the large muscle movements integrate with breath control and the body linkage connects rhythmically for fluid motion. The accompanying music on this section of DFS has a medium tempo with a strong underlying beat. The arms work through the torso, and various sequences are developed to focus on balance, coordination, and strength.

In summary, various physical components of flexibility, strength, coordination, agility, balance, and timing overlap in the training of both sport and dance. Athletes train specifically for those elements in their sport training but the dance experience focuses on a framework of sport similarity based on fundamental movements. Dance training provides a foundation for all movement focused on correct body mechanics, body awareness, postural alignment, body linkage, and fluidity in movement to enhance athletic performance. DFS is a great activity for all sports throughout the year whether in season or off-season. These simple sequences are ideal for athletes of all sports serving as an introduction to the perception of movements in dance. The skills of bending, stretching, and twisting are fundamental for sport skills allowing for the athlete to focus on sensations of these actions.

A POINT TO REMEMBER

Too often, these basic movements are overlooked.

Coaches and athletes work with more complicated movement patterns in action and gameplay specific to the sport and competition. DFS training highlights individual movement sense and proprioception in the fundamental training for the athlete. The dance experience is complementary to the sport training and is designed to enhance the athletic performance with adaptations to specific sports in the setting of a dance studio. The practice-based work of DFS is designed for athletes in preseason, off-season, and during the season. The simplicity of fundamental movement experiences is a foundation for all sports.

FEELING THE DANCE

/// 2 /// **FEELING THE DANCE**

Transfer of Training

Few areas of activity are literally transferable but dance comes the closest to any single training for all sports. Everything is about rhythm and the flow for the athlete in any sport.

Steve Miller, "godfather of Dance for Sports"

The importance of dance training for sport comes with the ability to transfer the dance skill back to the sport. The nature of the training needs to resemble conditions of a sport to influence the transfer of training to the performance of the athlete.[1] A similarity of fundamental movements in dance training reinforces the training to the specific sport. That is, the fundamental movements of bending, stretching, and twisting can be adapted to all sport skills. The ability of the athlete to translate the training and apply the skills to the specific sport competition and gameplay is an example of transfer of training. In this chapter, examples of fundamental exercises from DFS include the addition of rhythm and dynamics to the movement sequences for the athlete. The story of an Olympian and her transition from swimming to sculling presents a compelling illustration of transfer of training at the elite level. The arm action in the backstroke resembles the action of the oars in sculling.

Arm action has sport-specific skills and patterns, although similar mechanics and dynamics in movements exist. For example, pitchers in baseball and quarterbacks in football show similarity in the movements and mechanics of throwing actions. While the game situations differ between football and baseball, the biomechanics of the actual throwing motion of a baseball player and a quarterback are similar. The legs are crucial in the throwing action along with shoulder, hip strength, and rotational movement of the torso. The baseball pitcher maintains mental control to execute the pitch in baseball with repetition, consistency, and mechanics. The quarterback throws the football in game-play under the pressure of many unpredictable variables on the field with a time clock running. The rhythms and the dynamics of these two athletes are contrasted in gameplay, although similar in the action of the physical skill of throwing.

A baseball pitcher uses the same motion methodically, although the grip on the base-ball varies with the outcome to surprise the batter. In football, the quarterback uses the same grip on the football but the dynamics vary with his throwing motion and the nature of his pass, whether long or short. The sport specific outcomes result from the timing and control of the athletes in gameplay. Dynamics of a performance are specific to the sport with game situations influencing the throwing action. The simple exercises in this chapter introduce timing and control for individual performance, beneficial for sports on land or in the water.

Body awareness and timing are fundamental elements in both dance and sport contributing to a personal and intimate experience for the athlete. Physical abilities are personal traits that remain fundamental to the athlete in motor skill development. However, the transfer of motor skills is differentiated with physical abilities. The motor skill of throwing is distinguished from the physical expression of rhythm, a factor in the timing of movements. Use of rhythm is fundamental in motor skill development and piv-otal in the transfer of training. Rhythm is identified as the basis for movement technique and as the unique element necessary for a transfer of training in sport.[2]

THE ATHLETE'S STORY: FEELING THE DANCE

Caltech Athletic Director Betsy Mitchell is an Olympic champion (backstroke) swimmer. After completing her swimming career, she represented the United States in the World Sculling Championships in 1994. Betsy spent many years propelling her body in the water and transferred that skill to the boat and propelling on the water. The similarity of the action of the oars to the pull of the arms in the pool relates to mechanics. The biomechanics of the arm motion in the backstroke provide a long lever arm displacing the water and propelling the body through the water. Betsy found a similarity in the rhythms of the strokes of the oars pulling through the water to the arm strokes of the swimmer pulling through the water. Oars and arms are levers in the water propelling the competitor to the finish line in a linear path. The translation of the lever actions and cadence, whether in the water or on the water, led this Olympian to success.

Betsy Mitchell is a wonderful example in the transfer of training techniques from sport to sport. She transitioned successfully from a champion swimmer to a champion rower. Instinctively, she took to the water and went from competing *in the water* to competing *on the water*. She began rowing in a singles event and became a sprint champion and a member of the United States doubles team. The physiology of swimming and rowing are similar, as they both incorporate the total body and have intensive cardiovascular demands. Betsy finds rhythm in all the swimming strokes, specifically, the rhythm between the arm stroke and leg kick with rhythm of the six-beat kick or a two-beat kick. Every swimmer has to keep a constant rhythm and a personal tempo. The rhythm of the arms in the backstroke resembles the rhythm of the oars in water for the rower; thus, there is a similarity in the rhythm of the training for the athlete.

> In rowing, athletes in the boat must "feel the water" and "feel the boat." The rowers in the shell appear to be, "dancing on the water." The best rowing teams are in sync rhythmically through the economy of motion with an intramuscular ability to recover and transfer energy. If you enhance rhythmic ability, then you enhance rowing.
>
> Former USC and UCLA Rowing Coach Zenon Babraj

The synchronization of rowers in the boat is a visualization of the power of rhythm. Rowers feel a pulse in every stroke with their bodies, an example of kinesthetic awareness. The image of the rowers moving together in a steady pattern becomes a visualization of synchronicity in motion. The steady, consistent pattern merges the mechanical power of human bodies in motion with a fluid rhythmic action that is mesmerizing to the eye.

Betsy Mitchell illustrates the transfer of training with her ability to recognize a similarity in the patterns from swimming to rowing. For the athlete, the perception and internalization of basic rhythms becomes a gateway for rhythmic awareness. The athlete's adaptation of these patterns is the essence of motor skills and is essential in the transfer of training. Betsy's arms kept a rhythm in the water that transferred to the oars on the water.

A POINT TO REMEMBER

Rhythm is the unique variable transferable from sport to sport, dance to sport, and sport to dance.

A simple dance exercise sequence introduces the movement qualities of suspension, drop, and recovery, with a simple turn. The fundamental movements of bending, stretching, and twisting in this sequence are coupled with specific timing and counts. The timing creates the rhythm for the sequence that links movements together in fluid actions. The transfer of both movement qualities and timing enables an athlete to isolate the basic in action.

Body alignment and placement are introduced through the floor sequence and progress to a standing position. The dancer adapts the posture and alignment from the non-weight-bearing of the floor work to the upright weight-bearing position. Certain sequences of movement involve multiple muscle groups working together dynamically in varying dimensions with multiple forces and qualities. The fluidity of movement comes from the body linkage of the joint actions working together.

A POINT TO REMEMBER

The simplicity of elementary actions and movements must never be taken for granted in dance training.

DANCE FOR SPORTS IN PRACTICE: EXERCISES 5-7

DFS training links together the fundamental movements with rhythmic timing and specific movement sequences. These exercises encourage timing and concentration in simple pattern recognition.

EXERCISE 5: SUSPEND, TOSS, RELEASE, AND REBOUND STANDING CENTER FLOOR

The center floor exercises incorporate fundamental movements into a sequence of balance, rhythm, and body linkage. Facing the mirror, this introductory exercise begins with hips in a parallel position and feet slightly apart. This exercise works on the movement qualities of suspension, drop, and rebound.

(1) Begin with hips parallel and feet slightly apart as the right arm reaches upward and the body drops and suspends to the left (Count 1).
(2) The left arm tosses and extends upward (Count 2).
(3) The body releases and drops downward with knees bending (Count 3).
(4) Recovery rebounds upward to the center starting position (Count 4).
(5) Repeat the sequence to the opposite side.

Exercise 5 sequences are shown in Photos 2.1 to 2.4.

PHOTO 2.1. Standing with hips and feet parallel as right arm extends upward and body curves to suspend left (Count 1) *(Source/author: With permission from Rose Eichenbaum Photography)*

PERCEPTIONS: EXERCISE 5

- Experience the body linkage in suspension, drop, toss, and rebound.
- Sense the connection of the arms, torso, and breath throughout the movements.
- Feel the timing of counts 1, 2, 3, 4.

PHOTO 2.2. Left arm tosses upward toward the right arm (Count 2) *(Source/author: With permission from Rose Eichenbaum Photography)*

- Focus on the interdependent articulations of the torso, arms, head, and neck working together in synchronicity.
- Feel the impetus of continuous motion

SYNTHESIS TO SPORT: EXERCISE 5

- Forces and dynamics are controlled by the performer.
- Relate the posture, alignment, linkage, and awareness.
- Focus on arm movement connecting through the torso throughout the sequence.
- Body linkage connects through the torso in suspension.

PHOTO 2.3. Knees bend and body releases downward (Count 3) *(Source/author: With permission from Rose Eichenbaum Photography)*

- Simultaneous movements are linked by continuous motion.
- Fluidity is the result of the continuous motion.
- Experience the feeling of the torso release in drop and rebound.
- Let this become natural for adaptation in sport situations.

The next sequence adds a small lateral step to the standing sequence.

EXERCISE 6: SUSPEND, TOSS, RELEASE, AND REBOUND MOVING LATERALLY

(1) Begin with hips parallel and feet slightly apart; step to right on right foot (Count 1).

(2) Left arm tosses and extends upward (Count 2).

PHOTO 2.4. Recovery rebounds upward to center starting position (Count 4) *(Source/author: With permission from Rose Eichenbaum Photography)*

(3) Body releases and drops downward with knees bending (Count 3).

(4) Recovery rebounds upward to center starting position (Count 4).

(5) Repeat sequence to the opposite side.

Photo 2.5 illustrates Exercise 6.

PHOTO 2.5. Suspend left with hip parallel and step right with right arm extended upward and body curves *(Source/author: With permission from Rose Eichenbaum Photography)*

PERCEPTIONS: EXERCISE 6

- Involves weight transfer with lateral step.
- Spine remains straight into the floor as knees bend.
- Focus on hip flexors, hamstrings, and quadriceps.
- Movements of hip flexors are smooth and fluid.
- Experience timing through the entire motion.
- Maintain the alignment, body linkage, and breath control with the step.

SYNTHESIS TO SPORT: EXERCISE 6

- Establish straight postural alignment of the spine for body control.
- Ankle, foot, knee, and hip joints remain in alignment through movements.
- Rotation of hips joints increases range of movement.
- Use joint through range of movement and non-weight-bearing position
- Movements are fluid through continuous motion.
- Experience drop and recovery in one action.
- Maintain body control in suspension, step/toss, release, and rebound.
- Experience body control throughout movement sequence.

The next sequence adds a full turn with a small lateral step to the standing sequence.

EXERCISE 7: SUSPEND, TOSS, RELEASE, AND REBOUND LATERAL SEQUENT WITH TURN

(1) Begin with hips parallel and feet slightly apart; step to right on right foot (Count 1).
(2) Toss left arm to meet the right arm and execute a full turn in the same direction (Count 2).
(3) Body releases and drops downward with knees bending (Count 3).
(4) Recovery rebounds upward to center starting position (Count 4).
(5) Repeat sequence to the opposite side.

PERCEPTIONS: EXERCISE 7

- Execute a full turn in line of direction with the step.
- Establish balance and posture on a full turn.
- Experience a change of direction.
- Maintain postural alignment in standing position.
- Combine bending, stretching, and twisting of the torso in standing position.

- Establish and maintain balance on balls of the feet.
- Establish a fluid movement by connecting the actions and timing.
- Focus movements with the direction of the movement actions.

SYNTHESIS TO SPORT: EXERCISE 7

- Maintain body control with change of direction on full turn.
- Be aware of sensations of postural alignment in action.
- Control movement and balance through the toss and turn.
- Have sensations of connection of movement sequences.
- Control the body through actions of bending, stretching, and twisting.
- Transitions of actions emphasize the fluidity in movement.
- Balance is maintained over base of support as torso rotates.
- Recognize internal sensations and muscular control.
- Maintain focus on change of direction and turn.

REFLECTIONS FROM THE MIRROR

The fundamental movements are synchronized through specific timing with musical accompaniment in these exercise sequences. The recognition of the rhythm in movements is crucial for transfer of training in sport skills. The importance of proper placement and form aids in control of posture and alignment. These dance exercises introduce the athlete to rhythm and timing in the DFS work, with the music setting the tempo and mood. The center floor work aids in strength, balance, and coordination and builds on the fundamentals of bending, stretching, and twisting. With the athlete standing upright, this work engages large muscle movement integrated with breath control through the suspension and toss of the sequence. The release and rebound experience of letting go lets the athlete loosen the body and recover to the upright position. Music with a moderate tempo, neither too fast nor too slow, with a strong underlying beat aids to inspire both timing and mood for the exercises. The arms are incorporated and various sequences are developed to focus on balance, coordination, and strength. Any transfer to sport skill is enhanced by the fundamental skills, rhythms, and dynamics experienced by the athletes in DFS.

Athletes are encouraged to make adaptions in the transfer of skills from dance to their sport. These adaptations are natural for the athlete and should be recognized by the dance teacher.

Turns are often part of the movement sequences in DFS, and years ago, a student athlete taught me a lesson. When executing an outside turn that moves forward, one athlete kept executing an inside turn that moves backward. Although it was not the designated line of direction in the choreography, the athlete, a running back on the USC football team, continued with perfectly timed and executed inside turns. The execution of an inside turn was natural for the running back, especially during the football season. That running back was NFL star Reggie Bush. He demonstrated the necessity to turn away from the opponent to avoid being tackled or stripped of the ball in every game. Reggie executed inside turns in class, a natural action for a running back in football.. Clearly, he would never turn toward the opponent while carrying the ball but rather would turn away from the opponent. An inside turn was the maneuver he used on the playing field to avoid any interference in his gameplay and it became a natural movement in the dance studio. Movements are fluid when they follow a neuromuscular sequence that is natural for the performer. Reggie executed the turn in dance class similar to his actions on the football field with fluidity and seemingly effortless actions—beautiful to watch.

A POINT TO REMEMBER

Knowing the sport is important for both the dance teacher and the athlete because the dance should enhance the sport and not undo the sport skill. The success in this program hinges on the experience and knowledge of sport skills by the dance teacher and the adaptation by the athlete to the specific sport.

It is understandable that not every dance teacher may be an "accidental athlete" with thorough knowledge of sports, but the coaches can aid in the DFS education, too. Invite the dance teacher to attend practice to observe the skills and drills of your sport and to attend your competitions. DFS training recommends that the dance teacher and coach work together. The fundamental movements shared by dance and sport form in different ways with the various sports. The coach, athlete, and dance teacher work together to share the specifics of the training for the best adaptations of dance to sport. Form does follow function in sport, especially for the transfer of training to take place. Every sport has overriding patterns that athletes need to translate and transfer into their bodies.

Rhythm is a component in athletic performance and DFS supports the idea that the basic element transferable in sport is rhythm. This concept is identified as a unique variable in dance training. The significance of dance training for sport focuses on the understanding of specific timing and patterns in a variety of sports. In DFS, a dance teacher's broad-based understanding of many sport skills aids with identifying the similarities in dance and sport training to foster a transfer of training. The athletes' personal and intimate experience relies on both kinesthetic awareness and rhythmic awareness for the transfer of training in sport

HEARING THE DANCE

The Rhythmic Response

A successful triple jump can be heard even without being seen. The even audible sounds of the acceleration down the runway followed by the properly timed impact of the hop, followed by the step, the forceful accent of the jump on takeoff, and the final landing into the pit are unmistakable. The timing of a successful triple jump could be heard with your eyes closed or even with your back to the athlete.

Steve Miller, "godfather of Dance for Sports"

All movements follow rhythmic patterns whether in dance studios or athletic venues. These patterns of movement are seen, heard, and felt by the athlete, coach, and spectator. Athletes move through sport skills with specific timing and accents in movement sequences. This chapter finds examples from a variety of sports including swimming, track and field, and football. The task is finding the specific movement patterns in the sport and matching the sport-specific timing and accents with the athlete's personal awareness for a transfer of training. A positive transfer of training in motor skills and abilities is reinforced through rhythm.[1]

Rhythm, the result of linking patterns together at varying intervals in time, is an integral part of dance training. Dance exercises introduce the elements of underlying beats, accents, timing, tempo, and pace to the athletes through movement sequences with musical accompaniment. These musical elements establish the timing through patterns and repetitions in both sport and dance often via extrinsic or audible sound cues. The body responds to those cues while executing dance or sport skills, and this response becomes evident in sound, sight, or feelings. DFS establishes external rhythms with accompaniment and reinforces the internal response of the athletes through performance. Each sport finds distinct tempos to establish pace and patterns, both mental and physical, in practice and competition. The rhythmic training in dance alerts the performer to both external timing cues and the internal response to the cues.

> For example, "Symphony Kicking" is part of the swimmers' training at USC. The sounds of classical music establish the unique 30-minute training in the pool. The music breaks up the monotony in the workout and engages the swimmer with the ebbs and flows of soft and quiet music. The goal in this aquatic drill is for the swimmers to establish a rhythm with the tenor of the symphony music. The perfect musical accompaniment for the 500 meter race would be 4 minutes of music building to the crescendo.
>
> Olympic and USC Swimming Coach Dr. Dave Salo

THE ATHLETE'S STORY: HEARING THE DANCE

Olympian and track and field coach Jamie Nieto, two-time Olympian and four-time US high jump champion, identifies rhythm as the key to success in his performance. The combined effort of power, agility, and coordination of the high jump demonstrates the importance of timing on the approach, takeoff, jump, and landing. The high jump has a distinct rhythmic pattern from the drive to the takeoff, through the flight, to the landing. The entire jump takes only three seconds. Watching Jamie's Olympic jump, the rhythm is obvious: the sequence 1---2---3 4-5-6 (which is the cue to hit) and link to 7 (happening) 8 9 10 is both audible and visual. Jamie Nieto links the beats, accent, timing, and pace for a successful jump. His performance is smooth and the result is fluid movement with an understanding of timing, accent, and flow of the high jump. As Nieto said, "If you have to try too hard, it may be counterproductive. If you are smooth, the rhythm happens." The time intervals of the high jumpers' approach, takeoff, and flight are illustrated and measured in Figure 3.1 with simple lines.

In working with high jumpers, I often clap my hands, providing an audible rhythmic cue for the athlete. The pattern of the high jump is transcribed onto a musical staff with varying note values to reflect the acceleration and timing of the jump. The musical notes represent varying time values to mark a point in time, as shown in Figure 3.2. Thus, they illustrate the usual seven-step run, a quick step to precede the accented takeoff, and the accented penultimate step and landing. The quarter notes and eighth notes represent the time intervals of the steps for the high jump. Clapping the hands translates the steps of the jump as displayed by the notes and creates the rhythm of the high jump. These musical notes illustrate the timing of the steps described by Jamie Nieto and display the link between dance, sport, and music.

Time Intervals in a Line Pattern of the High Jump with lines indicated time intervals
By permission of Dr. Robert Cutietta, Dean USC Kaufman School of Dance and USC
Thornton School of Music

FIGURE 3.1. Time intervals in a line pattern of the high jump with lines indicating time intervals *(By permission of Dr. Robert Cutietta, Dean, USC Kaufman School of Dance and USC Thornton School of Music)*

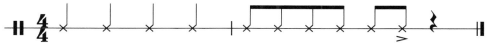

FIGURE 3.2. Musical staff and notation for the high jump *(By permission of Dr. Robert Cutietta, Dean, USC Kaufman School of Dance and USC Thornton School of Music)*

The high jump illustrates the fluid pattern of the beat, accent, and tempo to create a specific sport rhythm. A beat is the basic unit that is measured in time and establishes the pulse through repetition often referred to as the underlying beat, as in the acceleration of the jumper. The accent is the stress placed on a beat making it stronger or louder than the other beats. For example, the penultimate step is a slightly longer beat. The accent may be the downbeat for the dancer or the moment of takeoff for an athlete. The tempo will determine the pace. The beat, accent, and tempo are elements that become specific to particular sport skills. The coach's audible cues direct the rhythm of the race, becoming the accompaniment for the athlete. For the athlete, the task is to find the movement patterns in the sport to match his or her performance goals.

USC Track and Field Coach Caryl Smith Gilbert believes in vocalizing the "beeping" of a race or an event. "Beeping" is a combination of auditory and visualization techniques that she uses with the athletes. The athletes will quietly visualize and sound out their event by vocalizing a "Beep.". . . Beep.BEEP.BEEP.BEEP.BEEP, BEEP. The "beeps" reflect the speed, acceleration, and force, melding the sound and timing with verbalization of the sound of "Beep." Coach Caryl's vocalization illustrates the intensity and accelerating tempo in the rhythm of the movement patterns.

There is a rhythm in the competition for each event in track and field that an athlete locks in over 4–5 races. The more races that you run, the more fine-tuned the athlete becomes in that race. There is a "competition rhythm" that exists and is identified as coordination and kinesthetic awareness.

USC Track and Field Coach Caryl Smith Gilbert

Momentum is the effect of rhythm seen and felt in various sports. In many sports, the offense or defense may be surging or losing momentum on the court or on the field. Team sports like soccer, football, basketball, volleyball, and water polo carry momentum into each play. In football, the quarterback is the pivotal player and needs to feel the momentum of his teammates. However, eleven players have to find a mutual rhythm in the game of football.

A rhythm is created in the game in order for the quarterback to throw the ball on time. For example, the throwing time for a 15-yard pass has to be executed before the receiver actually turns to catch the ball. The quarterback has to feel the rhythm of his teammates and opponents, and the momentum of the game is seen, felt, and heard. The rhythms of an offense or a defense may result in a surge or loss of momentum on the field illustrating the mutual rhythm that the players need to find and maintain throughout the game.

Veteran NFL Coach Al Saunders

Both dance and sport work with the physical components of strength, speed, endurance, balance, and flexibility. The locomotor dance exercises in the next set reinforce rhythmic movement in various patterns and directions across the floor with musical accompaniment.

RESPONDING TO RHYTHM: EXERCISES 8–10

Dance step progressions move across the floor in single columns, usually four, with the first dancer in each line beginning the sequence, similar to sport drill formations. The progressions include the elements of weight transfer, change of direction, timing, agility, jumps, leaps, and turns with varying tempos and rhythmic patterns. These locomotor patterns synchronize steps, with music adding the external rhythmic cues. Fundamental step patterns reinforce varying time sequences in movement with even and uneven rhythmic patterns and step combinations, strengthening the rhythmic response. The athletes begin to identify specific rhythmic patterns, and this is vital in the transfer of training in dance and sport.

The teaching of fundamental dance skills consists of understanding the timing and subsequent weight transfer in movement and steps. The movements are broken down into both even and uneven counts with various tempos. With an even count, a movement is taken for each beat of the accompaniment. A simple even count is a steady movement pattern with a consistent beat: 1-2-3-4-5-6-7-8. An uneven count indicates a varied time pattern with a combination of slow and quick steps: 1-&2-3-&4-5-&6-7-&8 or a slow-quick/quick-slow-quick/quick-slow-quick/quick-slow-quick/quick. The movement patterns and counts may vary even further into something like: 1-&a2-3-&a4-5-&a6, 7-&a8, etc. The most important thing is for the performer to recognize the rhythm and identify the timing of the movement pattern in order to transfer that pattern into the movement action.

EXERCISE 8: LOCOMOTOR PROGRESSION WITH EVEN RHYTHM

A step pattern across the floor builds on the fundamentals to reinforce correct postural alignment, balance, and fluidity in movement, as outlined in DFS exercises 1–6. These progressions often begin with a simple walk across the floor to the rhythm of upbeat music with a moderate tempo. The athletes need only to stay with the underlying beat of the music and walk with their natural gait. This puts the beginner at ease in the dance studio setting and the teacher can begin to identify the student's individual styles. Dance elements and qualities are added to the walk, piece by piece, often giving the students an eight-count or sixteen-count improvisation of their own movement. In the locomotor sequences, athletes travel from one side of the studio to the opposite side and return to the original starting place. They generally adjust to this formation easily, as the organization resembles the formation in many drills similar to sport skill work.

This dance progression works with an even count, one step on each beat of the music, with changes in level and direction. Dancers begin the step with knees slightly bent on an even 1-2-3-4 count moving forward; then rising to the balls of the feet they continue a forward walk on even counts 5-6-7-8. A variation maintains the even count step pattern and adds a half turn. The step pattern moves forward on 1-2-3-4 with a half turn clockwise, followed by a walk stepping backward on 5-6-7-8. A clockwise half turn returns the dancer to forward direction.

(1) Begin on right foot and walk forward across studio on the even counts of 1-2-3-4 with knees slightly bent; then extend legs and rise to the balls of the feet and continue the even walk pattern on 5-6-7-8.
(2) Repeat the even count sequence on 1-2-3-4, adding a half turn clockwise and walk backward on counts 5-6-7-8, followed by a clockwise half turn.
(3) Repeat entire sequence on the left foot.

The pattern illustrates the rhythm of the step sequence in an even meter with one step on each beat depicted by the lines (see Figures 3.3 and 3.4).

▬ ▬ ▬ ▬ ▬ ▬ ▬ ▬

1   2   3   4   5   6   7   8

Time Intervals of Even Rhythmic Pattern 1-2-3-4-5-6-7-8

FIGURE 3.3. Time intervals of even rhythmic pattern 1-2-3-4 -5-6-7-8

L (step)
(Count 8)

R (step)
(Count 7)

L (step)
(Count 6)

R (step)
(Count 5)

L (step)
(Count 4)

R (step)
(Count 3)

L (step)
(Count 2)

R (step)
(Count 1)

FIGURE 3.4. Step pattern of even count walk (1-2-3-4-5-6-7-8)

PERCEPTIONS: EXERCISE 8

- Experience moving on the even beat of the rhythm.
- Experience bending, stretching, and turning on the beat in a locomotor sequence.
- Focus on timing, weight transfer, spatial directions, change of direction, change of levels, and maintaining step pattern on the beat of the sequence.
- Experience the timing of a turn in a locomotor pattern.

SYNTHESIS TO SPORT: EXERCISE 8

- Hear the external rhythm of the music.
- Match the internal rhythm of the athlete to the external rhythm of the music.
- Maintain the proper step pattern with an even rhythm.

- Add the bending and stretching into the even rhythm in a locomotor pattern.
- Execute a turn, while moving and maintaining the rhythm.
- Walk backward and maintain rhythm and body control

The next locomotor sequence travels from one side of the studio to the opposite side of the studio and introduces an uneven rhythmic pattern. It includes one step on the beat followed by a step-together-step moving with a change of direction to the corner. The timing of the step pattern adds an uneven rhythm or long, short, short step pattern. The step of one foot displacing the other is commonly known as a chasse in dance.

This progression builds with the even count on the walk forward—counts 1-2 with knees slightly bent—then it moves on a diagonal on counts 3&4. The sequence progresses in the forward direction on counts 5-6 and the opposite diagonal on 7&8. The timing is key as counts 3&4 and 7&8 are short, quick steps. The uneven step pattern alternates feet, as noted in Figure 3.5.

The pattern illustrates the uneven rhythm of the step sequence with one step on each beat depicted by the lines (see Figures 3.5–3.6).

EXERCISE 9: LOCOMOTOR PROGRESSION WITH UNEVEN RHYTHM

Begin on right foot and walk across studio on the sound of the underlying beat

(1) Walk two steps forward with knees slightly bent on an even count of step right on count 1 and left on 2.
(2) Walk diagonally to the right corner with an uneven count of step right on count 3 then left & right on &4.
(3) Repeat sequence to the left on counts 5-6-7&8.

PERCEPTIONS: EXERCISE 9

- Experience a change of direction to move on a diagonal.
- Identify the shift in timing from even to uneven.

```
■    ■    ■    ■■    ■    ■    ■    ■■
1    2    3    &4    5    6    7    &8
```

Time Intervals for uneven rhythmic pattern 1-2-3&4-5-6-7&8

FIGURE 3.5. Time intervals of uneven rhythmic pattern 1-2-3&4 -5-6-7&8

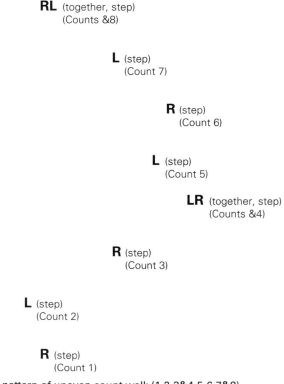

RL (together, step)
(Counts &8)

L (step)
(Count 7)

R (step)
(Count 6)

L (step)
(Count 5)

LR (together, step)
(Counts &4)

R (step)
(Count 3)

L (step)
(Count 2)

R (step)
(Count 1)

FIGURE 3.6. Step pattern of uneven count walk (1-2-3&4-5-6-7&8)

- Uneven timing affects the step size and duration: quicker steps of the &4 and &8 require smaller steps.
- Uneven timing results in alternating steps.
- Movement patterns remain smooth and fluid.

SYNTHESIS TO SPORT: EXERCISE 9

- Shifts in timing and direction are often used in gameplay.
- Establish timing with quick footwork.
- Maintain proper rhythm with weight transfer.
- Ankle, foot, knee, and hip joints remain in alignment through movements.
- Movements are fluid through continuous rhythmic motion.

A three-step turn is added to this locomotor sequence in an uneven rhythmic pattern. The progression builds off Exercise 8. The floor pattern moves forward and to the diagonal with the turn on counts 3&4 and 7&8. The feet come together on the turn providing a narrow base of support for the efficiency of the turn.

EXERCISE 10: LOCOMOTOR PROGRESSION WITH TURN

(1) Walk two steps forward with knees slightly bent on an even count of step right on count 1 and left on 2.

(2) Turn diagonally to the right corner with an uneven count of step right on count 3 then left and right on &4.

(3) Repeat sequence beginning forward with left on counts 5-6 and turn 7&8.

PERCEPTIONS: EXERCISE 10

- Experience a turn with a slight change of direction to move on a diagonal.
- Identify the shift in timing from even to uneven.
- Maintain visual focus on the turn by spotting[2] in the line of direction.
- Uneven timing affects the step sizes.
- Keep the rotation of the turn on the balls of the feet.
- Keep the turn tight with feet underneath the center of gravity.
- Quicker steps of the &4 and &8 require smaller steps.
- Keep movement patterns smooth and fluid.
- Establish and maintain balance on balls of the feet.
- Establish the fluid movement by connecting the actions.

SYNTHESIS TO SPORT: EXERCISE 10

- Be aware of turning in the line of direction.
- Feel the sensations of turning and maintaining balance.
- Experience the action and timing of turning.
- Experience the sensations of connection throughout movement sequences.
- Maintain control of body through the turn.
- Transitions of actions emphasize the fluidity in movement.
- Balance is maintained over base of support on the turn.
- Recognize internal sensations and muscular control.

REFLECTIONS FROM THE MIRROR

The rhythmic response to the music becomes visible in the performance of the athlete through the ability to hear and move to that rhythm. Obviously, sport competitions are not necessarily guided by musical accompaniment, but DFS allows the athlete to translate a rhythm into movement. The music provides a sound cue to reinforce and guide the timing, accent, and pace for movement. The dance training for athletes begins with working with an individual's ability to distinguish regular patterns of movement and or sound. An individual's rhythmic sense becomes a process of cognition in grouping a stimulus series into patterns. Dance movements accentuate an understanding of timing, accents, and fluidity gained through transitional links in continuous sequences and phrases. The sequences are taught in phrases through recall and reinforced through repetition.

The music inspires and creates both an energy and mood in the classes. The popular and current music in DFS provides steady beats. Usually, the musical accompaniment presents movements in segments in counts of 8 linked together into larger movement phrases. It is this measure of time and tempo that helps the dancer/athlete learn the movement patterns from simple to intricate by adding the new material in chunks of 8 counts. The exposure to the music in class promotes an opportunity for the student to identify the organization of the elements of time and force. Dancers/athletes identify their own movement sensations and their own timing. The task of the dance teacher is to help them find the rhythm and feelings within their own bodies.

Timing and controlling the motion of the segments of the human body contribute to fluid movement in a continuous path. Linking positions and movement points in space at intervals of time establishes rhythmic patterns. The essence of dance occurs within the transitions from point to point, with the body moving in fluid, efficient, effortless, and effective patterns through acceleration, deceleration, hesitation, or pause, creating a continuous path of motion. Both dance and sport train the human skeletal and muscular systems in similar ways to achieve their specific goals, as presented in Chapter 1 and Chapter 2.

In summary, all movement has a rhythmic pattern. The aim is to find the pattern to accompany your movement goal, be it dance or sport. In sport, the focus is on skills for the specific sport and competition. In dance, the focus of the motor skill activity is to work with the external and internal rhythms of the dancer. DFS is an effective tool in the training of athletes to find and transfer extrinsic and intrinsic beats and tempos in their own body into their sport. This personal and intimate experience of sound and feeling is dependent on kinesthetic awareness.

A POINT TO REMEMBER

It comes down to rhythm, from dance to sport or from sport to sport.

/// 4 /// POETRY IN MOTION

Kinesthetic Awareness

The ultimate control demonstrated in kinesthetic awareness may be with a body in flight; a dancer leaping in the air, a diver mid-air between the board and the water, or a jumper after takeoff and before landing on the ground. This demonstration of body control in the air is a true achievement of kinesthetic awareness.

Steve Miller, "godfather of Dance for Sports"

Kinesthetic awareness is the mind and body connection of knowing where your body is in space. This experience of body positioning is of particular importance to the dancer and the athlete. Proprioception, an aspect of kinesthetic awareness, is seen in the individual ability to perceive muscle motion, weight transfer, body position, and spatial orientation corresponding with body control, alignment, placement, posture, and balance. The kinesthetic sense influences these factors and works with the elements of force and direction in movement control. The effortless, efficient, and flawless movement in human performance is a result of this internal navigating sensation. Quite simply, being able to feel where your body is in space is not a skill that is taught but rather an experience demonstrated through performance. The performer does not move to make kinesthetic awareness happen but rather moves as a result of kinesthetic awareness.[1]

This chapter discusses kinesthetic awareness in various sports training conditions and competitive situations. The personal and intimate feelings of the performer contribute to this inner sense of individual awareness in location, movement, and forces. That awareness becomes evident in performance. Body control, alignment, placement, posture, and balance are factors working with the elements of force and direction in movement control in the various environments of sport competitions whether on land, in the air, or in the water. The DFS exercises work with aspects of proprioception through balance and control, as demonstrated with the exercises in this chapter. The perceptions of muscle movement, positions, and forces are experienced for adaptation to the environments and specific tasks in training and competition. DFS training highlights adaptations for these various sport environments.

The intimacy of finding one's kinesthetic sense is an internal ability based on an individual's personal feelings. In DFS, the dance teacher guides the student through experiences connecting with those internal sensations. The visible form of the performers becomes a representation of their feelings as demonstrated through their actions. The perception of movement and body position is of particular importance to the dancer and the athlete in the execution of movement skills.

A POINT TO REMEMBER

Clearly, the intimate feelings experienced by the performer are personal and cannot be taught, as the teacher never knows exactly what the performer is feeling.

The state of balance is an aspect of conditioning shared by both dance and sport, and the DFS exercises in this chapter work with equilibrium in both static and dynamic states. When a performer is off balance, this is felt by the performer and seen by the observer. In dance, fundamental movements train for balance by focusing on the individual's center of gravity. The control of the body in the air and in the water is a result of training on land enhanced through the DFS experience.

The pole vault is an example of the combination of forces, dynamics, and proprioception in an environment going from land to air. In executing the pole vault, the athlete must maintain balance at the top of the pole in order to project into flight. Running at full speed while carrying a fiberglass pole that is sixteen feet long and weighs five pounds is not a natural motion. The athlete accelerates down the runway to full speed, without the arm motion of a runner. The elements of speed, timing, balance, and courage are performance variables of this event in a successful jump. The body awareness needed to control the free flight over the bar is gained through training on land. DFS works with the elements of balance, postural alignment, and body linkage in movement to enhance the kinesthetic experience for the athlete on land, in the air, or in the water. The aquatic environment of sport poses a different environmental experience of kinesthetic awareness.

Balance in the water is different, yet an important variable in the symmetry of swimming. If a swimmer is "out of balance" in the water, the stroke will not be effective. Postural and core strength are essential for the efficiency of the swimmer. Kinesthetic awareness on dry land is different than in the water.

Olympic and USC Swim Coach Dr. Dave Salo

Body awareness is important to the swimmer, although the athletes are buoyant and non- weight-bearing in this sport. DFS recognizes this unique environmental training condition and provides a dry land approach to swim training. Elite swimmers present a challenge for the teacher in dance class. The swimmers need to adjust to working on land with weight-bearing and gravity-controlled movements after spending many hours buoyant and in water. The notion of finding one's "land legs" becomes necessary for the swimmers. In the dance studio, the aspects of weight-bearing movement, posture, balance, and weight transfer are important elements for the swimmer on land.

Kinesthetic awareness must be felt and become second nature. One of the most important postures in play is to establish the three points; that is, two legs for stabilization and one arm extended for throwing and catching. Water polo players train to throw, catch, and jump, while remaining buoyant in the water. The execution of these specific motor skills without the stability of solid ground is an extremely difficult task.

USC Water Polo Coach Jovan Vavic

The game of water polo presents a unique example of body awareness in athletic performance. These athletes remain buoyant and vertical for much of the game. The water polo player must master the ability to throw, catch, and jump without the loading advantage of a solid surface. The head and arms are visible throughout the game, and the motion of these aquatic stars often resembles a dancer's carriage of the arms or port de bras. Posture and core strength are important, especially for the players to remain vertical in the water. Catching and throwing a ball without their feet on the ground becomes a unique quality for these athletes. The body linkage of the water polo player is a masterpiece, with the body from the legs up through the core to the upper body and arms working together harmoniously.

The timing of this is crucial to coordinate the legs, core, and mind . . . thinking about the kinesthetic timing in such a fast-paced sport. Water polo is like "dancing in the water".

Stanford University Water Polo Coach John Vargas

THE ATHLETE'S STORY: FEELING THE DANCE

An athlete's technique and control of the body while running at top speed around the oval of the track is a vision of kinesthetic awareness. The mastery of movement results in efficiency, elegance, and grace. Today, Olympic gold medalist Quincy Watts is a USC track and field coach. In 1991, he was training for the Barcelona Olympic Games. He enrolled in modern dance class at USC to help his flexibility and body control. Quincy found dance a method of cross training different from his sport but providing fundamental movement similarities. His performances on the track and in the dance studio captured the essence of the term "poetry in motion." He moved with ease, power, and efficiency to master his sport. Quincy had the ability to make movement look easy by running 400 meters in 43.50 seconds with an almost effortless fluency and efficiency. In 1992, Quincy won the gold medal at the Barcelona Olympic Games in the 400 meter race and a second gold medal as part of the 1600 meter relay team. His coach describes him as "flying like a bird and soaring like an eagle." Watching this Olympian run is to see a vision of kinesthetic awareness.

Quincy describes running as demanding a focus on body control and speed, as his races of 100 meters, 200 meters, and 400 meters require powerful movement at varying speeds and consistent control and balance. Dance gave him a greater sense of body control and balance. He recalls the effortless feeling during his races and never experiencing fatigue. His personal state of being is impossible to measure and specific to his performance. Quincy describes the personal and intimate feelings that he experienced in the first heat of the Olympic qualifying race in Barcelona 1992. He felt the blend of the personal and intimate experiences of rhythmic awareness and kinesthetic awareness contributing to an optimal state of performance visible in his championship running.

Today, Coach Quincy Watts recommends dance as an excellent method of cross training for his young athletes. He finds that the fundamental movements of dance strengthen ligaments and tendons in a way very different from sport training. In dance, positions are held for strength and balance, focusing on body control. He remembers the value of dance from the plié, bending of the knees, and relevé, rising on the ball of the foot from the plié. Those simple dance sequences are important for strengthening the feet. As a sprinter, Quincy recalls that dance helped with the proper foot strike and action of coming through the ball of the foot. He still demonstrates the rise onto the balls of his feet in relevé to demonstrate the strike and roll through the ball of the foot in his running stride. He emphasizes striking on the ball of the foot and bringing that leg up underneath the body and the importance of specific foot actions in dance training. Sprinters tend to develop very tight ankles and Achilles tendons, and many of the stretching exercises in dance aid in loosening those tight, overused tendons, ligaments, and muscles. Breath control is also crucial to the runner and Quincy still practices the deep breathing exercises that are part of the dance warm-up featured in Chapter 1.

FINDING THE DANCE IN THE SPORT: EXERCISES 11–12

The following exercises work on both balance and proprioception. The athlete establishes their center of gravity and focuses on body awareness throughout these sequences.

EXERCISE 11: CENTER FLOOR PROPRIOCEPTION

(1) Stand on right leg with left leg bent, knees together, left heel high, and right arm overhead

(2) Left leg bends to a right angle next to the right knee; hips squared and facing forward with arms held overhead; leg extends forward with ankle extended and returns to starting position alternating ankle flexion and extension.

(3) Return to starting position and repeat entire sequence with left hip rotated outward in known in dance as *turn out* and leg extensions to the side for 8 counts.

(4) Ending pose with leg fully extended to the rear with toe pointed and leg extended known in dance as a low *arabesque* (Photos 4.1–4.4).

PERCEPTIONS: EXERCISE 11

* Experience the balance on a single supporting leg.
* Keep abdominal muscles engaged in upright posture.
* Find the center of gravity.
* Shift the center of gravity over supporting leg.
* Be aware of the difference in the parallel and turned-out positions.
* Experience flexion and extension in the balanced stance.
* Find and feel the full extension of the working leg to the rear.

SYNTHESIS TO SPORT: EXERCISE 11

* Find the center of gravity over the supporting leg.
* Maintain balance on one leg with the opposite knee bending and straightening.
* Maintain balance in the leg extensions to the front and to the side.
* Work the leg extension with hamstring and quadriceps muscles together.

PHOTO 4.1. Standing with hips parallel in a single leg stance *(Source/author: With permission from Rose Eichenbaum Photography)*

- Keep the rhythm of the movement with the external rhythm of the music.
- Engage the abdominal sheath for strength and control of the torso.
- Establish a sense of body awareness and feeling of movements.

PHOTO 4.2. Working leg extends forward with ankle alternating flexion and extension *(Source/author: With permission from Rose Eichenbaum Photography)*

The next exercise is a locomotor sequence that travels from one side of the studio to the opposite side of the studio and introduces an even rhythmic pattern combined with a hop in passé position and leg extended to the rear in a low arabesque. The hips remain turned out on the hop and rotated outward or turned out on the rear leg extension in the low arabesque. The hop takes off on one leg and lands on the same leg. The rhythmic count is on the even beat, one beat per step (Counts 1-2-3-4).

PHOTO 4.3. Repeat sequence with hips turned out and working leg to the side *(Source/author: With permission from Rose Eichenbaum Photography)*

EXERCISE 12: LOCOMOTOR PROGRESSION WITH THE HOP

(1) Moving forward on an even rhythm, beginning with right foot step right (Count1). Step left (Count 2). Step right Hop on right leg with left leg turned out to passé bent (Count 3). Land on left leg in *demi-plié* (Count 4). Alternate the sequence beginning on the left.

PHOTO 4.4. Ending position with working leg extended to the rear *(Source/author: With permission from Rose Eichenbaum Photography)*

(2) Moving forward on the even rhythm beginning with the right foot step right (Count 1), Step left (Count 2), Step right. Hop on right leg with left leg turned out hip and extended to the rear (arabesque)(Count 3). Land on left leg in demi plié (Count 4).

(3) Repeat beginning the entire sequence on the left foot (Photos 4.5–4.6).

PHOTO 4.5. Hop with hips turned out *(Source/author: With permission from Rose Eichenbaum Photography)*

PERCEPTIONS: EXERCISE 12

- Experience locomotor movement with body awareness.
- Use arms lifting upward on the parallel hop.
- Sense the difference in the body between the *parallel* and *turned out* positions of hips.

PHOTO 4.6. Hop with hips turned out and leg fully extended to the rear (low arabesque) *(Source/author: With permission from Rose Eichenbaum Photography)*

- Be aware of the use of arms in opposition on the turned out hop with leg extended to the rear.
- Feel the difference in the texture of the movements.
- Find and feel the full extension of the working leg to the rear.
- Establish a fluid movement by connecting the actions.

- Focus movements with the direction of the movement actions.
- Maintain body alignment and awareness in the air.
- Emphasize the *demi plié*, bending, on takeoff and landing from the ground

SYNTHESIS TO SPORT: EXERCISE 12

- Be aware of body posture and alignment over the center of gravity in locomotor movement.
- Be aware of changing hip placement during the sequence.
- Feel a movement of the body through recognition of internal sensations.
- Have cognitive awareness of the body movement.
- Maintain muscular control of body through space.
- Transitions of actions emphasize the fluidity in movement.
- Feel the sensations of continuity through movement sequences in a continuous path.
- Balance is maintained over base of support in the air on the hop.

REFLECTIONS FROM THE MIRROR

The mind/body connection of the athlete is enhanced with the development of body awareness in the dancer and the athlete. It is a motor-neural connection that is highlighted in dance training and in transitions of movements that connect to produce a smooth flow from point to point. The mind and body connect in ultimate performance through a personal and intimate experience for the performer in both dance and sport. The experience of timing and placement combine in a state of ultimate performance visible in the efficient, effortless movement.

In summary, dance allows for individual interpretation, providing a personal and intimate experience for the participant. The fact that feelings are connected to emotional expression is important in understanding the personal intimacy of the sense of body awareness in space. A person's feelings are the sensations that they experience internally. An individual's actions and movements are forms of their feelings made visible. Effortless, efficient, flawless movement and performance are the result of a blend of the rhythmic and kinesthetic awareness felt by the performer and seen by the observer. The dance training for the athlete identifies this individual sense of body awareness through balance, alignment, and the body linkage in movements. The personal and intimate sense of body awareness is always with the performer whether in the air, on land, or in water and is an aspect of sport specificity/similarity. The identification of the sensations or feelings of the body in space are tied with the patterns of movement.

Dance class reduces movements to finite elements such as breath, dimension, and quality of the action. The ultimate performance is a combination of rhythmic aware-ness and kinesthetic awareness, unique in dance training. The feeling or the awareness of the feeling remains intimate and personal only to the performer. The performance demonstrates that feeling of control, mastery, and joy in the movement. The spectator witnesses "poetry in motion."

Mind and Body Fitness

///5/// BETWEEN THE LINEAR AND THE LATERAL

Creativity and Improvisation

Coaches cannot remain at a standstill and must be creative and dynamic in seeking new ways to implement techniques of mechanics and training. It is important to leave room for creativity and improvisation and remain open for discovery in order to keep moving their sport forward.

Steve Miller, "godfather of Dance for Sports"

Competitive sport focuses on winning, often leaving little room for individual self-expression or interpretation. Strict training in sport works on techniques, training, rules, and regulations for a specific sport, limiting the creative experience for an athlete and leaving few opportunities for improvisation. However, athletes utilize creativity and improvisation in competitive situations through spontaneous adaptations specific for the offense or the defense in gameplay. Dance training develops the mind and body of the athlete in an atmosphere apart from competition.

This chapter looks at creativity and consequential improvisation for sport. Sport includes the strategies of the coaches and actions of the players with consequences in game situations. The coach's strategy establishes the game plan, while the athletes engage in the actions to carry out the plan in gameplay. Decision making, with immediate consequences, requires the individual athlete to adjust and act spontaneously in competitive situations. Simple examples of movement experiences in DFS training highlight the exploration of freedom in movement for the athlete, and the dance environment sets the stage for exploration in creativity and improvisation. Dance class promotes an atmosphere for mental focus and concentration by opening channels of self-discovery and exploration. DFS works to develop "consequential improvisation" for the athlete for spontaneous applications in gameplay.

THE DANCE ENVIRONMENT

The calmness of the dance studio presents an atmosphere very different from athletic settings. A change of venue and activity, a neutral setting without boundaries, serves to free the athlete's mind while he or she is moving the body, offering an opportunity for relaxation off the field. A dance studio with mirrors, ballet barres, and an open floor without impediments encourages freedom in movement. Musical accompaniment sets the mood in the studio. Simply enjoying "movement for the sake of movement" encourages self-discovery for the athlete by allowing him or her to find personal and individual expression. In dance classes, the freedom to explore creative possibilities is encouraged, often resulting in novel discoveries through movement experiences and a heightened sense of personal awareness.

> Dance classes were very relaxing before going to football practice and provided a state of calmness. Dance enhanced my abilities on the field and provided preventative rehabilitation for the care and prevention of injuries. Dance helped me tremendously to become a better athlete. The grind of football takes "all of you" and the athlete is consumed with structure from the weight room to the field. Dance is calming and reinforces free expression. Feelings are expressed through movement.
>
> Former USC and NFL player Lajuan Ramsey

CREATIVE COACHING

Applications of creativity and improvisation translate to sport, especially in competition and gameplay of various sports. The circumstances surrounding sport competitions include training, practice, and weather conditions often influencing creative and improvisational decisions. Actually, coaches in all sports are the choreographers, the athletes the dancers, and the game plans and strategies their choreography. The game plans and strategies, designed by the coaches and practiced by the players, represent platforms for creativity in sport. The creative edge comes into play when these plans take action in the game situation.

Football can be a choreographer's dream with eleven synchronized moving parts—all in expression of someone else's idea and never the same with all left to the interpretation. The screen passes are the most synchronized and choreographed plays in football, really poetry in motion. A beautiful sight when executed correctly. Big graceful athletes, all running in space with everyone moving in harmony and very little "close quarter contact." All moving in the open field in a graceful fashion becoming more about spatial relationships than brute strength.

NFL Veteran Coach Al Saunders

CREATIVITY IN ACTION

The athlete demonstrates creativity in carrying out the game strategy. UNC women's soccer coach Anson Dorrance recognizes creativity in the game of soccer, as the object is to deceive the opponent. The game is a maze of detail blended with simplicity in this fast-paced, nonstop sport demonstrating the need for "thinking with your feet." Dance requires the simultaneous processing of information of various visual and sound cues while the body is moving. To achieve this, a dancer must combine both rhythmic and kinesthetic awareness, the essence of dance training.

Creativity happens at the highest levels in the game of soccer. The only way that you can break down the defense is to think and move creatively in the game. Creative soccer players are artists.

UNC Soccer Coach Anson Dorrance

A POINT TO REMEMBER

Creativity cannot be taught as a skill but rather experienced as a way of thinking. The creative process is a form of problem solving that seeks novel solutions.

Dance class presents the conditions for developing creative and improvisational skills. Athletes explore the creative process in DFS through dance experiences via movement technique and choreography. Creativity is a process and the product is the resultant action whether in dance or sport. The combination of familiarity and variations results in the discovery of new movements. The games and activities present different environments and you cannot train for all possible conditions. Adaptations develop in the sport, as unplanned events result in a spontaneous, unrehearsed recovery for the athlete in competition.

> Football is a game of win or lose, right or wrong, good or bad. Football is a game of reaction, while dance is an activity of action. In football, the offense and the defense react to the action and in dance the performer initiates the action. "In dance, there is no such thing as right or wrong things are just true or false."
>
> Former USC and NFL athlete Thomas Williams

CREATING THE DANCE IN THE SPORT: EXERCISES 13–15

The exploration of creativity is an individual experience. Athletes follow rules, game plans, and strategies that often leave little room for individual expression. DFS offers opportunities for creative discovery. A few simple examples of creative exercises incorporate themes to guide the creative experience.

EXERCISE 13: INTERPRETING POETRY WITH MOVEMENT

(1) Each athlete is given a short poem to interpret through movement.
(2) Feelings replace words and words translate into movement.
(3) Begin without musical accompaniment.
(4) Musical accompaniment is later added to the movement.

EXERCISE 14: DANCING WITH AND WITHOUT AN OBJECT

This exercise incorporates a thematic structure of *ABA* (beginning, middle, end) to execute a movement plan.

(1) Movement with the object (A) represents the beginning.
(2) Movement without the object (B) represents the middle.
(3) Movement with the object (A) repeated represents the end.
(4) Musical accompaniment is selected by the athletes.

Examples of Exercise 14 are shown in Photos 5.1–5.4.

PHOTO 5.1. Athlete dance with a fencing foil (A) *(Source/author: With permission from Rose Eichenbaum Photography)*

EXERCISE 15: ABSTRACTION OF SPORT SKILLS

This exercise begins with the athlete's sport, although alternate sports are encouraged for exploration of creativity in action.

(1) Athletes take familiar sport movements and abstract the actions.
(2) They change the patterns and timing of sport movements.
(3) They change line of direction and interactions with sport movements.

Examples of Exercise 15 are shown in Photos 5.5–5.6.

PHOTO 5.2. Athlete with a fencing foil (A) *(Source/author: With permission from Rose Eichenbaum Photography)*

PERCEPTIONS: EXERCISES 13–15

- Explore the possibilities of new movements.
- Experience space, time, and shape variations through movement.
- Express ideas with movements.
- Express feeling with movements.

PHOTO 5.3. Athletes dance without the fencing foil (B) *(Source/author: With permission from Rose Eichenbaum Photography)*

- Individual expression is encouraged.
- Explore aspects of strategic creativity.

SYNTHESIS TO SPORT: EXERCISES 13–15

- Creativity relates to sport through tactical and creative opportunities.
- Explore tactical creativity with individual expression.
- Incorporate creative movement in sport movements.
- Athletes are free to explore their own movement possibilities.

PHOTO 5.4. Athletes dance with the fencing foil (A) *(Source/author: With permission from Rose Eichenbaum Photography)*

REFLECTIONS FROM THE MIRROR

DFS trains the individual athlete to consciously control movement. In dance, creativity becomes a way of thinking, an ability of the conscious mind expressed through movement. The guided experience in dance expands the movement vocabulary, knowledge, and self-awareness for the athlete. The new experience in dance encourages athletes to expand motor skills, cognitive skills, memory, and the language of movement outside the boundaries of sport. These exercises promote opportunities for free expression without rules, regulations, and scoring.

PHOTO 5.5. Dancer performs an abstraction from sports *(Source/author: With permission from Rose Eichenbaum Photography)*

A POINT TO REMEMBER

Creativity is a state of mind experienced by the athlete and demonstrated with actions in gameplay.

IMPROVISATION

Developing awareness of your body sensation; of the atmosphere, sound, air, light, everything that surrounds you; and of your inner instincts becomes a tool for improvisational

PHOTO 5.6.   Dancer performs an abstraction from sports *(Source/author: With permission from Rose Eichenbaum Photography)*

discovery. The internalization of technique matched with trust and instinct leads an athlete to move freely without constraints. The athlete reacts off the game plan, with changes in the competition and consequences. The action of improvisation in sport has consequences other than mere expression. The goal in DFS training is to develop a sense individual freedom in movement and creativity in mind to translate into movements of sequential improvisation: improvisation with consequences.

sport, improvisation is the result of spontaneity and an action of creativity. The ns of improvisation are unrehearsed and situation specific. The athlete needs to allow for this spontaneity and remain in control of the body. Various movement approaches offer the athlete improvisational experiences in DFS training. Those approaches include the locomotor approach, body movement approach, rhythmic approach, and spatial approach.

IMPROVISATION EXPLORATION FOR THE ATHLETE: EXERCISES 16–19

The following exercises allow the athlete to explore the freedom of movement and individual expression outside of sport. These experiences promote fun spontaneous action and response without consequences.

EXERCISE 16: BODY MOVEMENT APPROACH

(1) Explore movement patterns: isolate body parts.
(2) Explore change of direction: on audible cue, on motion cue.
(3) Experiment with movement qualities: ballistic, swinging, and sustained actions.
(4) Explore timing variations: fast to slow, start to stop, hesitation or pause.
(5) Experience movement abstraction: explore new variations of basic movements.

EXERCISE 17: LOCOMOTOR APPROACH

(1) Create variations of single fundamental steps: walk, run, skip, jump.
(2) Combine fundamental steps in variations: run-run-leap, step hop step leap.
(3) Practice change of direction on audible cue.
(4) Practice change of timing on audible cue.
(5) Experience freedom of expression and emotion in movement (see Photo 5.8).

Illustrations of Exercise 17 are shown in Photos 5.7–5.8.

EXERCISE 18: RHYTHMIC APPROACH COMBINED WITH SPATIAL APPROACH

(1) Perform a given movement pattern twice as fast or twice as slow as performed earlier.
(2) Perform actual sport movements at various tempos.
(3) Experiment with accent patterns and unexpected sound cues.
(4) Use varying tempo and movement speeds.
(5) Accelerate and decelerate the rhythm of the movement.

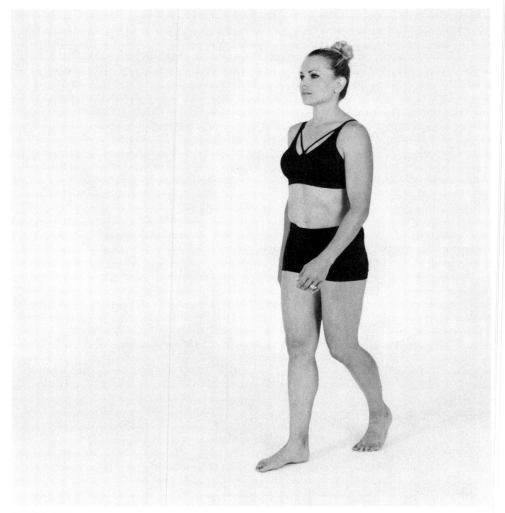

PHOTO 5.7. Basic walk locomotor pattern *(Source/author: With permission from Rose Eichenbaum Photography)*

EXERCISE 19: SPATIAL APPROACH

Experiment with reference to various floor patterns:

(1) Straight line patterns
(2) Curved line patterns
(3) Combination of straight and curved lines
(4) Symmetrical and asymmetrical patterns

PHOTO 5.8. Experience freedom of expression and emotion in movement *(Source/author: With permission from Rose Eichenbaum Photography)*

PERCEPTIONS: EXERCISES 16–19

- Experience discovery of new movements and formations.
- Explore space, time, and shape without restrictions.
- Experiment with change of direction, levels, and speed with movement.
- Explore qualities of movement through force and dynamics.
- Experience immediate response and spontaneous reaction.
- Express ideas with movements.
- Express feelings with movements.
- Explore abstraction in movement.

SYNTHESIS TO SPORT: EXERCISES 16–19

- Work together in small groups as a unit.
- Respond to situational timing and cues.
- Promote reaction time and response through verbal or musical cues.
- Explore creativity with individual expression.
- Incorporate creative movement in sport movements.
- Explore the capabilities of improvisation in movement.
- Incorporate body control in creativity and improvisation.

REFLECTIONS FROM THE MIRROR

Improvisation represents spontaneous movements often in relation to environmental circumstances. These unplanned actions are difficult to repeat or revise, as the situations vary. In dance, improvisation reflects feeling, emotions, and abstractions. In sport, improvisational movements have consequences. Creativity and improvisation in dance are expressive and often driven by emotion and feelings. These spontaneous and abstract skills apply to performance with the changing variables in the environment. The athlete and coach must respond and react with strategies, tactics, and consequences in gameplay.

Dance builds from basic movements into choreography and floor patterns. Improvisation encourages spontaneous movements of these fundamentals in unplanned actions. While creativity and improvisation in dance are expressive and often driven by emotion and feelings, the athlete utilizes these skills with strategy, actions, and consequences. Athletes and coaches respond and react with strategies, actions, and consequences to the changing variables in competitive situations. Creativity and improvisation are necessary skills for the spontaneous reactions to these changing sport environments.

CONSEQUENTIAL IMPROVISATION

Consequential improvisation is experienced by the athlete on the field, in practice, and in gameplay. Improvisational skills are difficult to repeat or revise, as the situations vary in the real time of gameplay. Anticipation and reaction are important factors coupled with motor skill abilities for optimal performance in sport situations. Those motor abilities include the physical components of strength, balance, coordination, and speed. The spontaneous reaction and response are the tools necessary for an improvisation experience. In dance training, the opportunities for spontaneity and experience allow a counterpoint to the linear drive and clock-driven pace of some sport training.

> The game plan is in a constant state of motion with many undetermined variables. Those variables may have been "rehearsed" at practice all week but change in the actual game. A quarterback executes an improvisation behind the line of scrimmage with the situation of missed blocks and rushing defenders. A quarterback "scramble" is an example of improvisation in gameplay as the quarterback stands on the field with the ball in hand looking for an opportunity. The many hours of practice cannot possibly capture the unanticipated plays that unfold in real time.
>
> NFL Veteran Coach Al Saunders

Coach Saunders confirms the importance of improvisation in football. Any notion of creativity must be strategic, and improvisation is strictly consequential. Coach Saunders's playbook has more than seven hundred pages full of plays planned with strategic creativity for the offense. Dance training does provide an introduction to improvisational skills, but in athletics any improvisation is best described as consequential improvisation. The strategic creativity of the coach guides the players on the field. The players engage in tactical creativity often resulting in consequential improvisation.

The highly organized nature of football training allows the athlete minimal opportunity for self-expression. NFL star Devon Kennard studied dance with me at USC. He is a linebacker for the New York Giants and was the 2014 Rookie of the Year. As a linebacker, he demonstrates the unique skills on the field of being an "airborne" back.

THE ATHLETE'S STORY: THINKING ON YOUR FEET

NFL linebacker Devon Kennard describes his ability to be in a state where all senses are engaged in the game: smell, feel, see, and hear at a high alert. The best games are those where the best rhythm flows. He defines flow is being "one" in the pace of the game and making all the right decisions. The unique skill of consequential improvisation is executed in the aerial or air-borne plays that lead to a tackle on landing. As a linebacker, he becomes airborne when he tackles, jumping over players and moving where the ball goes on the field. In the air, he must maintain control of his body and be balanced in his footing when he lands in order to react and tackle or move. The execution of this airborne tackling defense illustrates kinesthetic awareness at its best. He must be thinking while he is in the air and land with conviction and control to tackle this opponent.

In the game of football, an airborne defensive player has the ability to jump in the air, land, and tackle. Jump, land, and react is the plan. Devon uses an instinct to control his body in the air. If you land in an incorrect position, you can be hurt. Instinct is physically controlled with the strong core, as the center of control. The element of timing is crucial for the linebacker in football—knowing when to jump and not to jump. He needs an explosive action to get off the ground and must have the ability to maintain body control in the air. He must also have the instinct of knowing just when to use the airborne activity. Being in the air is being in a place of uncertainty, and the player must have an intent for immediate action upon landing.

Devon displays the aspects of creativity and consequential improvisation on the football field. His actions are the result of creative and competitive thinking. Creative thinking in sport is an adaptation of creativity in practice to competitive thinking in gameplay. The aspects of competitive thinking for the athlete include creative planning and action. The actualization of creativity is often implemented through improvisational movements in gameplay. The linebacker is a very rhythmic position on the defense. Linebackers are in the middle of everyone and must remain synchronized with the defensive line and the defensive backs. Devon indicates the defense must react by seeing, feeling, and hearing the action on the field.

In summary, dance training presents the athlete with experiences to foster creativity. Freedom of movement, with opportunities for self-expression, is enhanced through a personal state of awareness. The performer's body awareness, spatial awareness, sensitivity to time factors, and quick thinking are fundamental elements in improvisational movements. The basic physical components of strength, coordination, balance, flexibility, and agility need to be mastered to allow the body and mind to move freely. Improvisation develops the ability to adapt to the environment and to unknown people and to react to unexpected situations. Games and activities present different environments and you cannot train for all possible conditions. Adaptations must be developed on the spot.

> Creativity begins with the coach. The coach is the programmer of the workouts and cannot get locked into a system too tightly. Training should not be void of creativity. The athletes need variety in the workouts and without creativity and experimentation, things remain status quo.
>
> Steve Miller, "godfather" of Dance for Sports

Training of the athlete goes beyond physical training and perfection of technique. Coach Miller's insight was correct: "Few areas are literally transferable in sport but dance comes the closest." Everything is about the rhythm and the flow with fundamental movements being an individual focus. While the dancer moves to express feelings, the athlete uses feelings to direct movements. The intrinsic force of emotion for the dancer drives self-expression through movement. The extrinsic force of competition drives the emotion of the athlete to react and respond with movements in game situations. For the athlete, the movement has meaning and consequence, and for the dancer, the movement holds meaning and expression. The fundamental purpose of sport differs from that of dance, although the human body is the vehicle of performance.

A POINT TO REMEMBER

Dance is an art form of self-expression and abstract interpretation. Dance offers sport the opportunity for discovery and development of new movement possibilities through creativity and improvisation. Competitive thinking is a combination of creativity with the results including consequential improvisation in sport.

FORM, FUNCTION, AND FITNESS

Cross Training

It is important for coaches to incorporate activities that get the athletes off the field and just have fun. Cross training alleviates boredom and is valuable to athletes in all sports. Alternative activities are needed to reduce the effects of overtraining both physical and psychological for the athletes.

Steve Miller, "godfather of Dance for Sports"

For athletes at the elite levels of sport, the drills of strength training, conditioning, and stretching focus on specific sport skill training. And training is almost constant. An off-season is often difficult to define, as many athletes train almost all year with only an occasional day of rest; as a result, this intensity in the practice and competition of sports often leads to the fatigue of overtraining and to the potential for injury that can sideline the athlete. A viable solution is cross training. Cross training is exercise that makes the whole body stronger by combining several different activities. It is typically defined as engaging in alternate exercises or activities to improve fitness or performance in one's main sport.

A POINT TO REMEMBER

The best cross-training activities impact overall fitness, rehabilitation, overtraining tendencies, and psychological fatigue. A key to successful cross training is to find activities that can give joy and pleasure.

Dance offers a refreshing training approach to movement for the athlete. The benefit for training through the noncompetitive approach of dance training provides an alternative activity for both the body and the mind. This chapter highlights the value of dance as a movement experience for athletes, whether during the competitive or the off-season. In dance, athletes experience an individual awareness of movements by focusing on postural alignment, breath control, and muscular control. The dance exercises and actions allow for personal awareness and self-discovery in movements. Dance training works with the intrinsic value of personal experience, contrasting it with the extrinsic value of scoring and winning common in sport competitions. The common goals of core strength and body control are crucial for both athletes and dancers. An abdominal workout has become a signature feature in the DFS training of athletes. This chapter features this highly effective exercise sequence designed for strengthening the core in both dance and sport. Athletes from sports on the courts, on the track, and in the pool benefit from dance as a cross-training experience. Dance, as cross training for athletes, offers an enjoyable alternative to sport-specific drills. Athletes enjoy the fun of dancing while utilizing their bodies in different movement patterns.

Tennis is often thought of as an individual sport; however, the aspect of team camaraderie is essential at the collegiate level. USC Men's Tennis Coach Peter Smith maintains a joyful ambiance. His team enjoys hip-hop dance. A key to success for Coach Smith is to keep the athletes happy as they train diligently. The idea of a team dancing together brings harmony and unity to the group outside of the sport competition. The USC women's tennis team has also integrated dance into their off-season training. During preseason training, the lady Trojans enjoyed learning choreography in the dance studio following tennis practice.

Dance training includes a physical workout allowing the athletes to move beyond the boundaries of sport. The freedom of dance encourages natural expression and rhythm. The USC rowing team has studied dance in my classes. Dance training has helped these elite rowers maintain an extremely high level of endurance and strength as well as the smooth synchronicity of their movement rhythms.

As athletes, rowers are conditioned and prepared for the rigors of movement, and the natural rhythm in their bodies is perfect for dance. The adaptation to dance is natural for the rowers with an emphasis on synchronicity, rhythm, strength, and endurance. The linearity in the sport of rowing limits the athletes' range of movement and creative expression during competition. DFS provides opportunities for expanded muscle activity, encouraging individual discovery in the athlete.

Variety in training is important in the off-season with active participation in activities to prevent monotony in training. Dance provides a foundation for all sports.

Former USC and UCLA Rowing Coach Zenon Babjac

CORE STABILITY AND CORE STRENGTH

Core training, training of the abdominal sheath, is crucial in sport and dance performance. The focus of this training is powerful and precious—powerful, as the source of strength for most of our movements, especially in throwing and catching; and precious, as the abdominal muscles protect the vital organs of the human body. Coaches and trainers promote the importance of the abdominal sheath (core) in all sports. The strong multidimensional movements of the torso and abdominal muscles are essential in both dance and sport training.

The entire abdominal sheath is the base for multiple movement actions. These multidimensional movements in DFS reinforce the body linkage and are designed to strengthen this powerful musculature. The key to the effectiveness of this workout is the progression with continuous, rhythmic movement of breath and muscular action. The actions are detailed in Exercise 20, which is divided into three sections to be executed as a continuous sequence and accompanied with music. Three key body positions for each section are featured in the photos. A video of the entire abdominal workout is found in the Oxford University Press Companion website at www.oup.com/us/URL

EXERCISE 20: DFS ABDOMINAL WORKOUT

Part 1—Highlights lower abdominals

- Perform leg lifts and knee raises.
- Lift hips with feet parallel, feet crossed right over left, left over right, then parallel.
- Perform single leg reach with knee bent, then straight on right, left, both legs.
- With legs extended, ankles crossed right over left, left hand touches heel then reaches upward.
- With legs extended, ankles crossed left over right, right hand touches heel then reaches upward.
- Perform V-sit variation with arm press in parallel and turned-out hips.
- Execute a straddle right reach to side, center, upward.

Part 2—Highlights abdominal oblique

- Right leg extends straight upward knee to elbow, center inward, and straddle.
- Left leg extends straight upward knee to elbow, center inward, and straddle.
- Do double-time bicycle kicks with torso rotation.
- In slow tempo with ankles crossed and knees and feet at same level, alternate left elbow to right knee, right elbow to left knee.
- With right side only, turn out right hip, place foot below left knee.
- Bring left elbow to right knee.
- Lift left foot off floor, coming straight upward then across.
- Drop legs to side and come up on the oblique.
- Repeat sequence to left side and then oblique.

Part 3—Highlights rectus abdominals

- Sequence is performed from three difference positions.
- Head is cradled in the hands with abdominal lift upward in half time.
- Toes are together and heels lifted off the floor.
- Feet are flat and knees apart.
- Knees are together and feet apart.
- Arm variation through each position is added through center, to the side, and overhead.

Photos 6.1–6.3 show examples of positions for Exercise 12 sequence:
Part 1—Legs extended upward to highlight lower abdominals
Part 2—Twisting motion to highlight abdominal oblique
Part 3—Straight upward to highlight rectus abdominals

PERCEPTIONS: EXERCISE 20

- Entire abdominal sheath is worked through various sections.
- Part 1: Focus on the lower abdominals; keep legs elevated.
- Part 2: Focus on the abdominal oblique with twisting actions.
- Part 3: Focus on the rectus abdominal movement with feet in various positions.
- Head and neck remain relaxed.

PHOTO 6.1. Single leg reach with knee bent then straight on right, left, both legs *(Source/author: With permission from Rose Eichenbaum Photograph)*

- Exhale on the upward action.
- Maintain steady, natural breath flow.
- Actions are driven from the abdominal sheath throughout the sequence.

SYNTHESIS TO SPORT: EXERCISE 20

- Strengthening the abdominals relates to all movement.
- Incorporate natural breath rhythm into the sequence.
- Maintain postural alignment and awareness.
- Strong abdominals aid in injury prevention.
- Torso alignment and balance are reinforced.
- Concentrate on continuous, fluid movement.

PHOTO 6.2. Abdominal oblique with twist to right with turn out right hip place foot below left knee *(Source/author: With permission from Rose Eichenbaum Photography)*

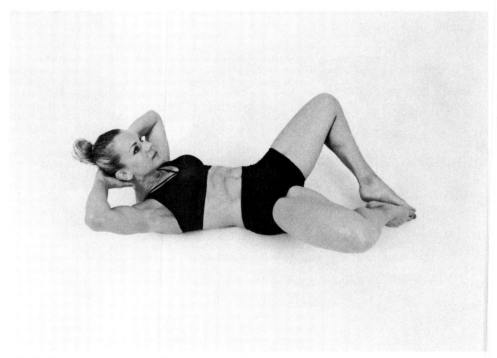

PHOTO 6.3. Rectus abdominal lift upward with head cradled in the hands *(Source/author: With permission from Rose Eichenbaum Photography)*

REFLECTIONS FROM THE MIRROR

The dance class focuses on abdominal awareness and control from warm-ups to choreography. Perhaps the most important article on the "core" was written decades ago in two simple pages titled "The Serape Effect."[1] The form and function of the abdominal sheath is illustrated with the image of a shawl or serape wrapped around the torso of the human body. The visual image of a "muscular serape" hanging over the shoulder, crossing on the anterior representing the four inner muscle groups, is concise and elegantly simple. The term "core" commonly refers to these muscles of the abdominal sheath, illustrated in Figure 6.1.

The serape image indicates the diagonal structure of these muscle groups working together. The forceful movement of the limbs in sport and dance tend to be diagonal in nature. The skills of throwing and kicking allow one limb to impart force to an object,

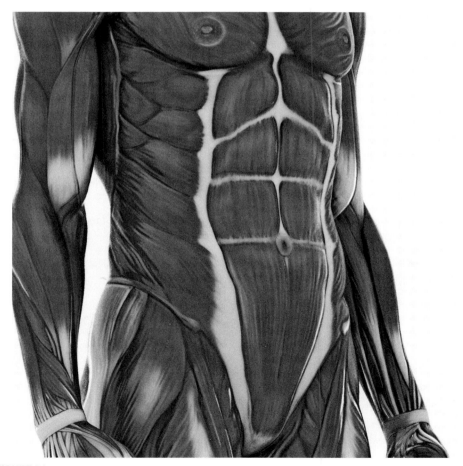

FIGURE 6.1. The abdominal sheath featuring the wrapping of the musculature in the torso *(Source/ author: With permission from Shutterstock.com)*

as the diagonal opposite limb engages to maintain balance with the performer in an up-right position. The posterior and anterior attachment controls force, action, and stabilization in the human body. The rhomboids and serratus anterior wrap from front to back with attachment at the vertebrae; the exterior oblique continues in a circular, downward direction on one side connecting into the internal oblique on the opposite side. The rhomboids have a downward and lateral direction and attach proximally to the spinal column and distally to the vertebral border of the scapula. The serratus anterior also attaches at the vertebral border of the scapula. The serratus anterior continues diagonally and downward as it attaches to the rib cage, both lateral and anterior. The internal oblique terminates at the pelvis.[2] The best way to think of this is to picture two diagonals crossing in the front of the body and working in conjunction with each other. The DFS abdominal work trains the muscles of entire abdominal sheath.

THE ATHLETE'S STORY: CONNECTING THE DOTS

Tatyana Obukhova McMahon is one of the USC strength and conditioning coaches and works with athletes in track and field, rowing, tennis, golf, and cross country. Tatyana was a USC student athlete from 1999 to 2003 and one of my dance students. She enrolled in dance classes for a cross-training experience. Tatyana masters fitness and body forms by merging the art and science of human movement. She views dance as a form of sport. Tatyana moves gracefully with an understanding of the fluidity in movement. She finds that dance promotes the continuous path of movements essential in the action of sport. Tatyana recommends dance for athletes as cross training. She finds activities in yoga more static, with poses and breathing not relevant to dynamics sports. Unlike the static poses of yoga, dance activities move in fluid paths that connect in space. The smooth, continuous movements and transitions of dance create the image of "connecting the dots" in space and time.

In dance class, Tatyana realized that the isolation of muscles and muscle groups gave her a better understanding of the mechanics of her own body. In dance, it is possible to slow things down and focus on finite movements that athletes do not often have time to discover. Dance works with alignment and flexibility, especially important to athletes. Through dance training, Tatyana learned to relax her entire body to relieve the tightness in specific muscles. The strong core training provides the stabilization for fluid movement in all directions and rotations, whatever the application—dance or sport. She recommends that athletes study dance in their off-season for maximum enjoyment and fulfillment.

Dance training provides alternative stretches and relaxation for overworked muscle groups. Conditioning for athletes often focuses on strength training in the weight room for running, jumping, and throwing. DFS offers a variety in the training. For example, runners need to achieve and maintain flexibility that is often overlooked with the linear training that they must do for their events. The openness of dance class offers movement in various lines of direction rather than merely linear point to point. In dance, the element of time varies and the runner is provided opportunities to move at varying time intervals and not always in a linear direction at top speed.

The benefits of dance training for track and field athletes are particularly important even during the competitive season. The repetition and linearity of movement in practice and competition result in an obvious tightness in athletes' hip flexors; the alternate movements of dance, using other muscles, help to relieve this stress. The athletes can enjoy the opportunity to engage in dance and choreography between championship competitions without interference with their running techniques.

The dry land training in DFS offers an alternative approach for athletes in water-engaged sports. Water polo players possess a unique ability to throw and catch the ball without the use of their feet on the ground. This particular skill demonstrates incredible abdominal strength with control of the upper body and limbs. In dance, the shoulder stability and carriage of the arms works the arms from the chest muscles of the pectoralis major and pectoralis minor with the latissimus dorsi of the back. This subtle movement contrasts the grasping from the larger trapezius and deltoid muscles as prime movers often used in sport.

A constant reciprocal relationship between flexion and extension of alternate limbs, both upper and lower, is seen in many sport skills. The dynamic stabilization function of the external and internal oblique muscles is probably more important for upper and lower limb movements.[3] The "serape effect" illustrates the function and importance of the interrelationship between the pelvic girdle and rib cage action when upper and lower limbs are used in ballistic action, such as throwing and catching.

In summary, athletes spend the majority of their practice time in drills and game plans with the focus on competition. Alternative activities are needed to reduce the effects of both physical and psychological overtraining. Dance focuses on fundamental movement in a setting that is very different from sport. The coach and the dance teacher work together for an enjoyable and effective cross-training experience. The specific training of the abdominal sheath, carriage of the arms, use of the upper body, breath control, and postural alignment are values of DFS training.

Beyond the Dance

/// 7 ///　ARÊTE

Body and Spirit in Pure Symmetry

I see sport as a multidisciplinary experience, not only physical but psychological and emotional. The width and breadth of movement and competition cannot be defined singularly.

Steve Miller, "godfather of Dance for Sports"

For over thirty years, the majority of my work with athletes in dance classes was conducted at the University of Southern California in a dance studio located in the physical education building. The Ancient Greek words of Plato are inscribed in concrete outside that building:

Ανθρωπος ψυχη και σωμα συμμετρος

Man should have harmony in both soul and body or should be equally cultivating soul and body.[1]

These words refer to the fine tuning of the human body to achieve a pure symmetry, a balance of body and soul. An athlete's personal and intimate experience in performance results from the internal connection of the mind, body, and spirit in balance. The performance becomes a visualization of the personal rhythm and harmony of the athlete. DFS training reaches beyond technique and skill to help athletes experience this personal balance through self-discovery, as they begin to identify the feelings behind their movements and actions.

Dance introduces the opportunity for athletes to connect the mind, body, and spirit in performance. Skills and drills work with the physical development of the athlete but

95

dance allows time to think about a broader dimension of athletic performance: the totality of mind, body, and spirit. This chapter shows how DFS expands the thinking about dance and sport from practical to philosophical, with reflection on the themes of the body and soul in relation to dance and sport training with a look at sport in Ancient Greece. The concept of Arête brings together the mind, body, and spirit in physical training.

ARÊTE

Arête, a rather illusive term, is defined in early Greek civilization by excellence and is difficult to translate into English.[2] Plato uses this term in reference to athletic training and education and best depicts perfection in athleticism. Arête connects to athleticism, broadening the definition to include virtue, skill, prowess, pride, excellence, valor, and nobility.[3] This intangible element is said to be in the mind, body, and spirit of great athletes and to performance in the Olympic games. Arête refers to emotional and intellectual excellence and pride manifested through honorable physical actions. If an individual believes arête has been achieved, then arête is actually lost. The fleeting goal of excellence is a constant state to be sought. The never-ending search pushes the individual to become better.

To say arête depicts excellence and virtue is an incomplete definition. Arête is beyond the scope of materialism and greater than mere excellence. The term excellence often refers to material objects. Arête is the epitome of being and a culmination of traits such as kindness, care for others, beauty, rhythm, and aesthetics. The magnitude of this concept with relation to human performance and fulfilling one's full potential dates back to the Homeric years. In fact, Arête, the goddess or personified spirit of virtue, excellence, goodness, and valor, visited selected newborn babies to offer them her blessing. This is myth, but it leads to the notion that true arête with reference to athletic performance may be God-given or spiritual. The Ancient Greeks believed that dance was actually a gift from the twelve gods. They included the element of charisma into the notion of arête, noting that arête is truly a gift, one that may be based on heredity. That is, some are born to be great athletes. Each person of arête was held to reach the highest level of effectiveness, utilizing all their faculties. Olympic diver, Greg Louganis, embodies arête in both sport and life. Greg Louganis appears to have this special gift.

Professor and former National Rowing Coach for Greece and the UK

Dr. Yiannis Koutedakis

THE ATHLETE'S STORY: ARÊTE

Olympic Diving Coach Ron O'Brien finds that "excellence is the constant pursuit of a goal."⁴ O'Brien coached Olympic champion Greg Louganis. Together, they demonstrated the meaning of arête. Greg Louganis may be the greatest diver to ever compete at the highest level of sport. Aesthetics and athleticism combine in his performance. This diver defined the elements of beauty, strength, grace, agility, timing, fluidity, efficiency, and rhythm. The diving of Greg Louganis exemplifies the elegance of the human body in motion. The timing and rhythm of his diving actions unfolding midair provide a visual connection between dance and sport. To watch Greg dive is to see "ballet in the air." Coach O'Brien describes the beauty and pure symmetry of Greg's diving as presenting the illusion of effortless movement.

Kinesthetic awareness, rhythmic awareness, and their subsequent balance (pure symmetry) are the contributing factors to effortless movement. The performance of a trained dancer often appears as effortless beauty, as a dancer is trained to move efficiently using grace, timing, rhythm, and fluidity in the movements. Diving, as a competitive sport, compacts a high level of concentration and skill into characteristically small but finely tuned movements. The diver's space is bound by the limits of the narrow diving board. He or she follows an invisible path in free flight before entering a target area in the pool. The temporal quality of the dive is also limited by spatial bounds, with the prescribed path of the dive taking a certain amount of time to complete. From the moment of takeoff, through the free flight, and to the moment of entry, time becomes relative to the observer and the diver. The dive cannot be savored, for it passes and vanishes too quickly. The element of kinesthetic awareness may best be shown in the body of a diver in the air.

The Ancient Greeks valued the total development of the athlete by blending art and science, work and play, mind and body in society and sport. To Aristotle, the health of the mind was dependent on the health of the body, linking both art and science throughout his works. Health and virtue contribute to this balance and become necessary elements in achieving the pure symmetry of body and spirit. Plato's *Republic*, Book IV, discusses the elements of rhythm and harmony both in society and individual actions for athletes. Athletes held a powerful role in society beyond competitions and contests and were held in high esteem by the Ancient Greeks. Their training included a balance of mind, body, and spirit to benefit the individual and the state with expectation that they would become exemplary citizens.

A POINT TO REMEMBER

Education of the physical and education through the physical were common themes in Ancient Greece.

> Dance offers an enriched movement vocabulary to all competitors. Dance allows for individual movement and reinforces fundamental movements by breaking down movement patterns into simple steps and rhythms.
>
> Professor and former National Rowing Coach for Greece and the UK
>
> Dr. Yiannis Koutedakis

The educational experience of dance reaches a dimension of self-discovery beyond the physical and expanding to the intellectual and emotional dimensions of an individual. The fundamental movements of dance provide a vehicle for training the athlete to reach beyond physical movement by relating feeling to movement, connecting the mind, body, and spirit. DFS allows for experiences in the artistic and creative aspects of movement. In dance, emotions are expressed through movement with a creative abstraction of ideas and feelings. Dance frees athletes to explore individual feelings, allowing them to connect with sensations of the body in space and to sharpen body awareness related to their movement capabilities. These experiences become a sensation owned by an individual, truly a personal and intimate experience. The feelings are important to overall performance, especially from the aspect of kinesthetic awareness.

Dance training for the athlete is an individual experience, although it may be shared with a group. The idea of a united body, mind, and spirit is rooted in Ancient Greek society, as demonstrated by the Olympic athletes in training, performance, and stature. Dance training for athletes addresses rhythm and harmony for each individual athlete and in the union of the team, enhanced by music that provides an upbeat element. Athletes enjoy the fun of dancing while utilizing their bodies in different movement patterns. The unity of the teams sharing a dance experience in the dance studio creates a harmonious atmosphere for the team, essential to the camaraderie in sport.

In summary, an education through dance offers the athlete an opportunity for personal exploration of body movement based on anatomy, physiology, and psychology. Dancers experience a motor-neural connection, a synthesis of feelings and actions in movement. Both athletes and dancers work to perfect technique, although in dance the mechanical aspects of movement are coupled with feelings and emotion. Movement in dance represents the union of intellectual processes with personal experience and values. In sport, the personal experience and values are demonstrated through fair play and teamwork. While the elements of coordination, flexibility, strength, and endurance are emphasized in training procedures for both dance and sport, specific rhythmic training is integrated in the process of dance training. In dance, the internal and external rhythms between the dancer and music are integral to the training.

The practice of DFS provides the opportunity for athletes to pursue intellectual mastery of the body through enjoyable activities. The integration of cognitive knowledge and physical control enhances their ability to express their unique ideas. Intellectual, emotional, and spiritual elements are synthesized and internalized, becoming vital for dynamic movement. This synthesis begins the early development of arête in the athlete. To achieve arête is constantly beyond reach, thus promoting a state of constant growth for an individual.

The pure symmetry of body and spirit is part of a duality that echoes in DFS. The mind/body element is enhanced with the development of kinesthetic and rhythmic awareness in the dancer and the athlete. Training in dance strives for a motor-neural connection that produces fluid movements flowing seamlessly from point to point. The mind and body connect in performance that becomes a personal and intimate experience for the performer in both dance and sport.

> Now, as we were saying, isn't it a mixture of musical and physical training that makes these elements: concordant, tightening and nurturing the first with the fine words and learning, while relaxing, soothing, and making gentle the second by means of harmony and rhythm?
>
> Socrates from Plato's *Republic*, Book 4[5]

DANCE FOR DIVERS

The introduction to dance for divers begins with the basic concepts of movement articulations in a sequence of exercises with divers lying supine on the floor; it progresses to the ballet barre and center floor work. Progressions across the floor and excerpts of simple choreography add spatial awareness, cognitive work, and essentially fun to the workout. A relaxing cool-down ends the class in preparation for training.

Part 1—Body Awareness and Alignment (lying on the floor)

(a) Overall stretch and vertebral alignment.
(b) Rib-cage breathing to emphasize breath control.
(c) Contraction and release of the abdominals to emphasize control of the body center or core.
(d) Leg bending and extension for hip flexors in parallel position and turned out position.
(e) Articulation of the feet through plantar flexion and dorsi flexion.

After body awareness and alignment, placement is introduced to divers through the floor sequence in Part I. The next progression follows to a standing position at the ballet barre, then progresses with divers facing the mirrors in center floor.

Part II—Ballet Barre Work Progressing to Center Floor Sequence for Strength and Balance

(a) Pliés—An exercise in dance for strength, balance, and vertical alignment, usually a warm-up for the hips, legs, feet, and ankles with simple bending. Traditional ballet positions (first through fifth position of the feet) with turned out hip and parallel hip variations.

A Point to Remember: The sport of diving works with parallel hips and the turned out exercise works to increase the range of movement in tight hip joints.

    (a) Plié Sequence
        (i)   two demi pliés.
        (ii) one grand plié.
        (iii) plié, relevé, straighten up, lower down.
        (iv) relevé, plié, heels down, straighten legs.
        (v)   turned out position—first, second, fourth, fifth.
    (b) End in relevé position—rising to half toe through extension of foot and ankles which aids in balance.

A Point to Remember: The relevé position is characteristic of the divers' preparation at the end of the diving board.

    (c) Port de Bras—carriage of the arms.

        Arm movements in dance work from underneath through the latissimus dorsi and pectorals rather than using deltoid and trapezius muscles as the primary movers. The dance training works to enhance the aesthetic alignment and reduces tension in the shoulders and neck by working muscularly from underneath rather than from the upper musculature.

A Point to Remember: The use of the arms is important in diving, and hyperextension of the elbows is a common problem.

    (d) Tendu—small brushes of the feet on the floor emphasizing plantar flexion.
    (e) Dégagé—small brushes of the feet off the floor emphasizing plantar flexion.

Combination of tendu and dégagé into a brush, release, balance, contract/drop, and recover.

    (f) Attitude swings (front, side, back, side to second position plié and side stretch) to warm up hip flexors with easy swings and knee bent.
    (g) Grand Battement—large leg beat with straight leg to release hip flexors.

The basic stretch sequence was taught center floor facing the mirrors in small segments with musical accompaniment in a 4/4 meter with a moderate to fast tempo. This work emphasizes strength and balance for the divers, while linking movements into a series of stretches.

Part III—Center Floor Standing Stretches

1. Standing Stretches
    (a) Achilles stretch with arms overhead (add lunge).
    (b) Overhead stretch and reach; extend forward to flat back.
    (c) Flat back lengthening spine: right, left, center, back.
    (d) Side stretches with back extension and torso twist.
    (e) Twist, toss, drop, circle.
    (g) Achilles and psoas stretch (add torso twist).
    (h) Plié and pull through (second position).
    (i) Arm circle, plié and reach, contract up.

The purpose of this segment is to emphasize the changes of direction in space and weight and to transfer body weight with relation to the performance space. The locomotor patterns are designed to synchronize steps with music, integrate rhythmic perception, and combine the dimensions of space and time with movement sequences across the floor.

The locomotor sequences include the basic steps of walk, run, step-hop, pivot-turn, jumps (one-foot and two-foot takeoff to a two-foot landing) in a variety of combinations with changing tempo and directions. This section is designed to expand the elements of space and time for the divers in addition to adding an element of fun.

A Point to Remember: The divers' performance space is limited to the narrow diving board, small platform, and aerial movement with the aquatic element defining the entry into the water.

Part IV—Movements across the Floor (Locomotor)

1. Basic walk with variations of tempo and levels.
2. Step-hop in variation of timing and body position.
3. Simple runs in plié.
4. Basic turns combined with various step patterns.
5. Simple jumps with quarter turn, half turn, and full turn.

A cool-down ends the class, as the athletes relax and prepare for their training.

A slow sequence of stretches with divers seated on the floor and facing the mirrors: continuing gentle stretch, body linkage, and kinesthetic awareness. The musical accompaniment of a slow tempo intends to quiet the mind and body.

Part V—Cool-Down Center Floor (facing mirrors)

1. Seated position
   (a) Cross-sit position; quietly gathering body energies in the body center and lengthening through the spine.
   (b) Upper back extends with a torso twist with focus front.
   (c) Stretches to the side alternating right, left, and circle around.
   (d) Hip release; add upward extension; add sideward full body extension.
   (e) Long sit with stretch and upper back extension, flat back to curve.
   (f) Straddle stretch with contraction over leg and side stretch.
   (h) Bent leg straddle and Sartorius stretch
2. Lying on Floor in Supine Position
   (a) Single leg resistance stretch for hamstrings.
   (b) Rond de jambe of leg.
   (c) Flexion and extension of knee and ankle joint.
   (d) Stretch to split or half split.
   (e) V-sits (pike position).
   (f) Deep breathing in supine position.

CONVERSATIONS WITH CHAMPIONS

The following individuals were interviewed in research for *Dance for Sports*; they are listed by sport or topic:

ARÊTE
Dr. C. L. "Max" Nikias, President, University of Southern California

BASEBALL
Dan Hubbs, USC Coach

BASKETBALL
Andy Enfield, USC Coach

BOXING
Gerald Washington, Former NFL and USC Football Player

DIVING
Hongping Li, Olympian and USC Coach
Greg Louganis, Olympian
Dr. Rick Schavone, Retired Stanford Coach

FOOTBALL
Pat Haden, Former NFL and USC Athlete and Former Athletic Director
Patrick "Birdie" Hall, Former USC Athlete
Devon Kennard, NFL Athlete and Former USC Athlete
John Martinez, Former USC Athlete
Kennedy Polamalu, UCLA Coach
LaJuan Ramsey, Former NFL and USC Athlete
Al Saunders, Veteran NFL Coach
Lynn Swann, Former NFL and USC Athletic Director
Thomas Williams, Former NFL and USC Athlete

LACROSSE
Lindsey Munday, USC Coach
Joe Romano, Bellermine Prep Athletic Director

ROWING
Zenon Babraj, Former USC and UCLA Coach
Anita DeFranz, Olympian
Dr. Yiannis Koutedakis, Former British and Greek National Rowing Coach

SOCCER
Anson Dorrance, University of North Carolina Coach
Keidane McAlpine, USC Coach

SWIMMING
Oussama Mellouli, Olympian
Betsy Mitchell, Olympian and Caltech Athletic Director
Dr. Dave Salo, USC Coach

TENNIS
Dick Gould, Stanford Director of Tennis
Tim Mayotte, Champion Athlete and Coach
Peter Smith, USC Coach

TRACK AND FIELD
Ron Allice, Former USC Coach
Sheldon Blockburger, USC Coach
Brooks Johnson, Olympic and Former Stanford Coach
Late Peyton Jordan (letters), Former Olympic/Stanford/USC Coach and Athlete
Denis Kholev, Former USC Athlete
Tatyana Obukhova McMahon, USC Coach and Former USC Athlete
Steve Miller, Agassi Graf Foundation (Foreword)
Jamie Nieto, Olympian
Caryl Smith Gilbert, USC Coach
Quincy Watts, USC Coach

WATER POLO
Dante Dettamanti, Retired Stanford Coach
Kostas Genidounias, Olympian
John Vargas, Stanford Coach
Jovan Vavic, USC Coach

VOLLEYBALL
Mick Haley, USC Coach
Paula Weishoff, Olympian and Coach, Concordia University

GLOSSARY OF TERMS IN DANCE, SPORT, AND ANATOMY

DANCE TERMINOLOGY

ABA   Structure for choreography including a theme and variation into a beginning (A), middle (B), and end (A).

Arabesque   Body supported on one leg with other leg straight and extended to the rear with the height of the rear leg either low or high.

Attitude   Leg in the air is bent at the knee.

Ballet Barre   A stationary rail utilized in dance as an apparatus to aid in alignment, posture, balance, and symmetry for technique and training.

Ballet Fifth Position of the Arms   Arms extended above the head, slightly forward with elbows slightly bent and hands apart.

Ballet Second Position of the Arms   Arms extended to the side with elbows below the shoulders, and wrist below the elbows.

Chasse   One foot displaces the other in a quick gliding step.

Degage   Leg moves off the floor with pointed foot and straight leg.

Demi Plié   Knees bend halfway with heels staying on the ground.

Floor Work   A sequence of exercises done while lying on the floor either in supine or prone position.

Grand Battement   Leg extends from the hip into the air and moves back to original position.

Inside Turn   A turn backward or away from the line of direction.

Outside turn   A turn moving forward in the line of direction.

Parallel Position of the Hips   Standing position without hip rotation.

Passé   Leg is raised and bent at the knee placed near the knee of the supporting leg.

Port de Bras   The carriage of the arms in dance.

Releve   Rising to balance on the ball of the foot.

Rond de Jambe   Leg moves in a series of circular movements on the ground or in the air.

Suspension   A dance movement resembling a dangling position that hangs from above allowing for free movement.

Tendu   Stretching of foot and leg with foot while keeping foot on the floor.

Turn out   Outward rotation of the leg coming from the hip joint.

SPORT TERMINOLOGY

6-4-3 Double Play   A play in baseball initiated by the shortstop. Shortstop (6) fields the ball and throws the ball to the second baseman (4) for the first out; the second baseman throws the ball to the first baseman (3) for the second out; scored as 6-4-3.

Penultimate Step   Second to the last step prior to the takeoff in jumping.

Quarterback Scramble   Impromptu actions of the quarterback when under pressure behind the line of scrimmage.

Sculling   The sport of rowing in a small, narrow boat for one, two, or four people.

Six Beat Kick   A swimming kick pattern that propels the swimmer forward with momentum. The timing is counted with one-two-three—one-two-three or Right—two-three—Left-two-three. The beats are synchronized with the arm patterns.

Sport   A contest or game in which people engage in physical activities in accordance with a specific set of rules in either team or individual competition.

Two Beat Kick   A two-beat kick pattern, which mimics a six-beat pattern, although more economical with fewer kicks. This is a symmetrical pattern with two kicks for each arm stroke requiring more balance for the swimmer.

ANATOMY TERMINOLOGY

Abdominal Oblique   Muscles from the anterior and lateral abdominal wall.

Abdominal Sheath   Posterior and anterior sheaths made of the muscles fibers of the abdominal muscles.

Core   The abdominal sheath in the body.

Deltoid   Triangular shaped muscle at upper part of the arm and top of the shoulder.

Dorsiflexion   Backward flexion (bending).

External Oblique   Largest and most superficial muscles of the lateral anterior abdomen.

Gluteal Muscles   Muscles of the buttocks.

Hamstrings   Any of three muscles located in the back of the thigh.

Hip Flexors   Several muscles that bring legs and trunk together in flexion movement

Internal Oblique   Muscle of the abdominal wall below the external oblique and above the transverse abdominal muscles.

Inward Rotation   Turning about axis of rotation toward midline of the body.

Latissimus Dorsi   Large, flat muscle of the back that stretches to the sides of the torso.

Outward Rotation   Turning about the axis of rotation away from the midline of the body.

Pectoralis Major   Muscle of the chest (anterior).

Pectoralis Minor   Muscles of the chest beneath the pectoralis major.

Plantar Flexion   Movement of foot with toes flexed downward (extending).

Psoas   Long muscle on the side of the lumbar region and the top of the pelvis.

Quadriceps   Group of muscles located in the front of the thigh.

Rectus Abdominal   A paired muscle running vertical on each side of the anterior abdominal wall.

Rhomboids   Muscles associated with scapula located on each side of upper back.

Sartorius   Longest muscle of the human body found in the anterior thigh.

Serratus Anterior   Muscle origin on the surface of the first to eighth ribs.

Supine   Lying horizontal with torso facing upward.

Trapezius   One of the major muscles of the back covering upper back and posterior neck.

NOTES

THE BACKSTORY

1. Ali, *The Soul of a Butterfly*, p. 72.

CHAPTER 1

1. Wessel, *Movement Fundamentals*, p. 85.

CHAPTER 2

1. Gamble, *Strength and Conditioning for Team Sports*, p. 1.
2. Bondarchuk, *Transfer of Training in Sports*, p. 180.

CHAPTER 3

1. Bondarchuk, *Transfer of Training in Sports*, p. 180.
2. Focus of the head and eyes to maintain a constant orientation for control and to avoid dizziness.

CHAPTER 4

1. Howard Gardner, email, September 12, 2014:

   I would say that 'being aware of your body and its options' is quintessential to bodily-kinesthetic (b-k) intelligence. The only hitch is that the awareness need not be conscious, and certainly not hyper-conscious. In other words, b-k intelligence manifests itself whether or not the person can speak about it or conceptualize it. I'd say the same thing about any intelligence. The test is in performance-per-se, not in self-awareness or articulateness.

CHAPTER 6

1. Logan and McKinney, "The Serape Effect."
2. Logan and McKinney, "The Serape Effect."
3. Logan and McKinney, "The Serape Effect."

CHAPTER 7

1. Yannis Yortsos, dean, USC Viterbi School of Engineering, translation of Plato's words.
2. Cahill, *Sailing the Wine-Dark Sea*, p. 12.
3. Miller, *Arête*, p. 107.
4. Furjanic and Sweeney, *Back on Board: Greg Louganis* (A Documentary Film).
5. Plato, *Republic*, p. 130.

BIBLIOGRAPHY

Ali, Muhammad. *The Soul of a Butterfly*. New York: Simon and Schuster, 2004.

Bondarchuk, Anatoliy P. *Transfer of Training in Sports*. Translated from the Russian by Michael Yessis. Muskegon Heights, MI: Ultimate Athletic Concepts, 2007.

Cahill, Thomas. *Sailing the Wine-Dark Sea*. New York: Doubleday, 2003.

Furjanic, Cheryl, Filmmaker and Producer, and Producer Will Sweeney. *Back on Board: Greg Louganis* (A Documentary Film), 2014.

Gamble, Paul. *Strength and Conditioning for Team Sports*. London: Routledge, 2010.

Leonard, George. *The Ultimate Athlete*. New York: Avon, 1974.

Logan, E. A., and C. McKinney. "The Serape Effect." *Journal of Health, Physical Education and Recreation* 41, no. 2 (1970): 79.

Miller, Stephen G. *Arête*. Berkeley: University of California Press, 2004.

Plato. *Republic*. Translated from New Standard Greek text by C. D. C. Reeve. Indianapolis: Hackett, 2004.

Wessel, Janet. *Movement Fundamentals*. Englewood Cliffs, NJ: Prentice-Hall, 1961.

FURTHER READINGS

BACKSTORY

Gallwey, W. Timothy. *The Inner Game of Tennis: The Classic Guide to the Mental Side of Peak Performance.* New York: Random House, 2008.

CHAPTER 1

Epstein, David. *The Sports Gene: Inside the Science of Extraordinary Athletic Performance.* New York: Penguin Group, 2014.

CHAPTER 2

Jackson, Susan A., and Mihaly Csikszentmihalyi. *Flow in Sports: The Keys to Optimal Experiences and Performances.* Champaign, IL: Human Kinetics, 1999.

CHAPTER 3

Brown, Daniel James. *Boys in the Boat: Nine Americans and Their Epic Quest for Gold at the 1936 Berlin Olympics.* New York: Penguin Books, 2013.

Levitin, Daniel J. *This Is Your Brain on Music: The Science of Human Obsession.* New York: Penguin Group, 2007.

CHAPTER 4

Gardner, Howard. *Frames of Mind: The Theory of Multiple Intelligences.* New York: Basic Books, 1983.

CHAPTER 5

Blasing, Bettina, and Thomas Schack, editors. *The Neurocognition of Dance, Mind, Movement, and Motor Skills.* New York: Taylor & Francis, 2010.

Damasio, Antonio. *The Feeling of What Happens: Body Emotion in the Making of Consciousness.* New York: Harcourt, 1999.

Memmert, Daniel. *Teaching Tactical Creativity in Sport: Research and Practice.* London: Routledge, 2015.

CHAPTER 6

Koutedakis, Yiannis, and N. C. Craig Sharp. *The Fit and Healthy Dancer.* West Sussex, England: John Wiley, 1999.

CHAPTER 7

Aristotle. *Poetics.* Cambridge, MA: Harvard University Press, 1995.

Golden, Mark. *Sport and Society in Ancient Greece.* New York: Cambridge University Press, 2003.

Lewis, Michael. *COACH: Lessons on the Game of Life.* New York: W. W. Norton, 2005.

NAME INDEX

SUBJECT INDEX